SCIENCE

and the

MIND

of the

M*A*KER

SCIENCE
and the
MIND
of the
MAKER

MELISSA CAIN TRAVIS

HARVEST HOUSE PUBLISHERS
EUGENE, OREGON

All Scripture quotations are from The ESV® Bible (The Holy Bible, English Standard Version®), copyright © 2001 by Crossway, a publishing ministry of Good News Publishers. Used by permission. All rights reserved.

Cover by Bryce Williamson

Cover photos © ilbusca, wetcake, mustafahacalaki, STILLFX / iStockphoto; Gena96 / Shutterstock

Image on page 123: Wikimedia Commons, RNA-comparedto-DNAthymineAndUracilCorrected .png.

Image on page 159: Image ID: 50392971. Copyright Tomas Kovalcik, Dreamstime.com, http:// dreamstime.com/tomkovalcik_info. Used with permission.

Science and the Mind of the Maker
Copyright © 2018 Melissa Cain Travis
Published by Harvest House Publishers
Eugene, Oregon 97408
www.harvesthousepublishers.com

ISBN 978-0-7369-7128-7 (pbk.)
ISBN 978-0-7369-7129-4 (eBook)

Library of Congress Cataloging-in-Publication Data is on file at the Library of Congress, Washington, DC.

Printed in the United States of America

18 19 20 21 22 23 24 25 26 / VP-GL / 10 9 8 7 6 5 4 3 2 1

To Jonathan, Corban, and Cayden

Acknowledgments

To my husband Jonathan, all my love and appreciation for your emotional and practical support, without which this project would have been impossible.

Special thanks is due to my dear friend and colleague Dr. Holly Ordway, for her invaluable advice and guidance throughout my writing process.

My sincere gratitude to the following scholars for their reading and critique of specific chapters: Dr. Guillermo Gonzalez, Dr. Mark Linville, Kevin Wong, Brandon Rickabaugh, Carolina Liskey, Hillary Ferrer, and Wes Skolits.

Heartfelt thanks to wonderful friends who offered insightful manuscript feedback and much needed prayers and words of encouragement: Julie Miller, Ken Mann, Jason Kline, and Jenny Courville.

For their faithful prayers and continual moral support, my deep appreciation to Reverend Lisa Schwandt, Bishop Clark Lowenfield, Terri Washburn, and Alison Strobel Morrow.

Most importantly, I am thankful to my Lord Jesus Christ, who is always faithful in carrying me through the challenges of the work he gives me to do. *Soli Deo gloria.*

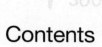

Contents

Thou that fill'st our waiting eyes
With the food of contemplation,
Setting in thy darkened skies
Signs of infinite creation,
Grant to nightly meditation
What the toilsome day denies—
Teach me in this earthly station
Heavenly Truth to realise.

• • • • • • • •

Through the creatures Thou hast made
Show the brightness of Thy glory,
Be eternal Truth displayed
In their substance transitory,
Till green Earth and Ocean hoary,
Mossy rock and tender blade
Tell the same unending story—
"We are Truth in Form arrayed."

James Clerk Maxwell
A Student's Evening Hymn
Cambridge, 1853

Prologue:
Science as the Experience of a Masterpiece

*God invents the truth of the universe,
as his art; man discovers it, as his science.
Human science is the indirect reading of the divine mind.*[1]
Peter Kreeft

Science is a marvelous enterprise. It expands our knowledge of the world around us, illuminating the macroscopic, the microscopic, and even some of the altogether unseen. Human ingenuity has produced everything from space telescopes that capture breathtaking, high-definition images of galaxies hundreds of thousands of light-years in diameter and millions of light-years away to functional nanomachines composed of only a few molecules. In countless respects, scientific discovery has vastly improved the human condition through advances in medicine, agriculture, transportation, and communication. We are rightfully awestruck by science's ability to explain the workings of the universe and enhance the quality of our lives.

Yet profound questions inevitably arise from what we're learning about nature and our capacity for understanding it: Why does anything exist at all? What was the ultimate cause of all things? Why is there a deep rationality in nature that corresponds to the human intellect? Why are our minds trustworthy finders of complex, abstract truths, such as those gleaned through logic and the advanced mathematics employed by the sciences? These kinds of questions transcend the domain of science and require interaction with philosophy and theology. Note, however, that the answers these two disciplines provide do not, in any way, undermine the natural sciences. In fact, philosophical and theological insights significantly enhance our understanding of why science is possible in the first place. Oxford philosopher Richard Swinburne has a clever way of phrasing this idea: "I do not deny that science explains, but I postulate God to explain why science explains. The very success of science in showing us how deeply orderly the natural world is provides strong grounds for believing that there is an even deeper cause of that order."[2]

That's what this book is about—how Christian theism uniquely provides a well-rounded account of both the findings and the existence of the natural sciences. I will argue that not only do scientific discoveries have positive implications for the existence of a Mind behind the universe, they strongly suggest that this Mind intended for human beings to take up the noble project of rational inquiry into the mysteries of nature. In other words, Christian theism, unlike atheism, offers a sufficient explanation of the observable features of the natural world as well as mankind's impressive scientific achievements.

The title of this book intentionally echoes the words of Dorothy Sayers, a theologian, novelist, and playwright who explored the relationship between literary artists and the doctrine of the Trinity in her book *The Mind of the Maker*. In a passage that immediately captured my imagination, Sayers wrote, "As soon as the mind of the maker has been made manifest in a work, a way of communication is established between other minds and his."[3] Indeed! In stories, poetry, musical compositions, and visual art, the creator of a piece shares his or her thoughts with all those who experience his or her creations; contemplation of a work allows us to gain a glimpse into the mind of the artist. Upon reading Sayers's words, it occurred to me that this is certainly true of the most magnificent of all creations—the cosmos. Our world is a masterpiece that can be appreciated both aesthetically and intellectually; this includes scientific exploration as well as philosophical and theological reflection.

Two astonishing facts make scientific activity possible: the fundamental rationality of nature, and the existence of inquisitive creatures with intellects fit to discern that rationality. Why are things this way? Atheistic materialism—the view that nothing exists beyond the material world—must treat this uncanny resonance as nothing more than inexplicable happenstance. Yet the fact that we inhabit an orderly universe structured in such a way that the human mind can grasp it to a remarkable degree is exactly what we should expect if there is a Maker of all things in whose image we are made and whose mind is made manifest in the rest of creation.

I call this the Maker Thesis.

Chapter 1

The Science and Faith Conversation: Understanding the Lay of the Land

> One of the great achievements of science has been, if not to make it impossible for intelligent people to be religious, then at least to make it possible for them not to be religious. We should not retreat from this accomplishment.[1]
>
> *Stephen Weinberg*

> I never said a word against eminent men of science. What I complain of is a vague popular philosophy which supposes itself to be scientific when it is really nothing but a sort of new religion...[2]
>
> *G.K. Chesterton*

Religion and science are engaged in a kind of war: a war for understanding, a war about whether we should have good reasons for what we accept as true...I see this as only one battle in a wider war—a war between rationality and superstition."[3]

So says Jerry Coyne, a University of Chicago evolutionary biologist and bestselling author, in his diatribe against religious belief, *Faith vs. Fact: Why Science and Religion are Incompatible.* Despite the fact that he is untrained in either philosophy or theology, Coyne spends nearly 300 pages attempting to support his philosophical claim that religion is incapable of finding out truth and that science is the only form of rational inquiry that is "capable of describing and understanding reality."[4] He describes the alleged war between science and religion as one between evidence-based reason and groundless superstition. He defines *truth* and *fact* as "what exists in reality and can be verified by rational and independent observers."[5] Coyne believes that this excludes divine revelation and the existence of God. Moreover, he regards human beings as fully material creatures, dismissing the concept of an immortal soul as "a superfluous religious add-on" to proper science.[6]

Coyne's book is only one among many recent presentations of the science-therefore-no-God narrative. About a year prior to the publication of *Faith vs. Fact*, a major media outlet released a critically acclaimed reboot of atheist cosmologist Carl Sagan's 1980 miniseries, *Cosmos: A Personal Voyage*. Hosted by Dr. Neil deGrasse Tyson, professor of astrophysics at Princeton University and popular science personality, *Cosmos: A Spacetime Odyssey* is a visually stunning exhibition of our universe that, quite rightfully, inspires an acute sense of awe and wonder. The implicit message is, "Look how amazing the cosmos is and consider how powerful science is, to have unlocked so many of its mysteries!" Certainly most viewers would readily agree, regardless of their religious persuasion.

Unfortunately, *Cosmos* goes beyond the actual science and implies answers to more fundamental questions about reality, such as mankind's place in the universe and whether or not anything exists *beyond* the material realm. The very first episode features a clip from the opening sequence of the original version of *Cosmos*, including Sagan's famous statement: "The cosmos is all that is, or ever was, or ever will be." This sets up a philosophical framework in which the physical stuff of the world—matter and energy—is all that exists, a paradigm that automatically excludes a transcendent Creator and an immaterial human soul. In this view, there is no mindful plan behind the universe; blind, naturalistic processes alone must be sufficient to explain everything. This ideological undercurrent pervades the remainder of the series; the vastness of space and the cosmic timescale are strongly emphasized in order to reinforce that we are "little guys living on a speck of dust afloat in a staggering immensity"[7] of space and time. *Cosmos* was nominated for 12 Emmy Awards and was renewed for a second season, which is slated for release in 2019.

Yet another example, one that has sparked a flurry of fresh scholarly debate in recent years, came from Stephen Hawking, who was perhaps the most celebrated theoretical physicist and cosmologist of our day, and Leonard Mlodinow, a theoretical physicist turned popular science writer. In their book *The Grand Design*, Hawking and Mlodinow declared that "philosophy is dead," and therefore, questions about the nature of ultimate reality now fall entirely within the domain of science. "Scientists," they explained, "have become the bearers of the torch of discovery in our quest for knowledge," and advancements in physics and cosmology "lead us to a new picture of the universe and our place in it that is very different from the traditional one."[8] By "traditional" they presumably mean religious. Hawking and Mlodinow concluded that God is, in fact, not required for explaining the cosmos, which "can and will create itself out of nothing" thanks to the laws of nature. After publication, *The Grand Design* shot to the number one position on the New York Times Best Sellers list.

This is a small but representative sampling of the steady stream of "science versus faith" rhetoric saturating our culture through the channels of popular-level science books, articles, and documentaries written or endorsed by celebrities of the scientific community. We are informed by the "experts" that the advancements of modern science have rendered God superfluous; that invoking a supernatural agent or other spiritual entities to account for our universe, living things, and human nature is completely unnecessary. Sure, there remain a few unanswered questions, but (according to their view) science will eventually fill in the finer details, providing fully naturalistic explanations for all of reality. We are told that there is no longer any need to resort to medieval superstition in order to have a virtually comprehensive understanding of the world, and anyone who claims otherwise is either scientifically illiterate or suffering from some kind of religion-induced delusion. It's time, they say, for religious people to wake up and face the fact that we humans are merely the self-aware material by-products of a blindly evolving universe, and there's not a shred of evidence to support the existence of a creator God, much less one who had us in mind.

Some Philosophical Considerations

The Oxford mathematician and science and religion scholar Dr. John Lennox is fond of saying, "Statements made by scientists are not always statements of science." It's a pithy remark that reminds us to carefully scrutinize the pronouncements of credentialed scientists and draw a distinction between genuinely *scientific* statements and philosophical statements made *about* science. In the earlier examples from popular-level science media, we can identify a few major philosophical presuppositions: naturalism, materialism, and scientism.

Naturalism is the inherently atheistic worldview that excludes the existence of God and conceives of the universe as a closed, self-contained system that—at least in principle—can be fully described using naturalistic explanations. Sagan's iconic statement about the cosmos being all that exists is a perfect expression of this view. Nearly all naturalists embrace *materialism*, which says that everything in the cosmos is, or can be reduced to, matter and energy governed by the laws of nature. Technically, it is possible to be a materialist without denying the existence of God, but many people, including most nonacademics, use the term in a decidedly atheistic sense. Therefore, going forward, my use of the word *materialism* should be understood to include naturalism.

Scientism (hard scientism, to be precise) is the view that science has a monopoly on the rational pursuit of knowledge—that we can only know to be true what science has demonstrated, and anything science cannot methodically examine cannot be known to exist.[9] For example, thanks to the science of chemistry, we know that water is composed of two hydrogen atoms bonded to an oxygen atom. However, a transcendent Creator responsible for the laws of physics and chemistry and the existence of those atoms is inaccessible by the various empirical methods of science and thus cannot be considered part of reality.

The main problem with scientism is that it is self-refuting (it contradicts itself), and a self-refuting statement is always false. For example, suppose someone were to say to you, "There are no true statements in the English language." That person has automatically defeated his own statement, for he uttered it in English. Similarly, the claim "We can only know to be true what science shows to be true" cannot itself be shown to be true by way of scientific investigation, because it is a philosophical statement. The inherent contradiction is inescapable.

So in attempting to negate all other methods of obtaining knowledge about the world (philosophical reflection or divine revelation, for example), scientism shoots itself in the foot. Moreover, scientism's claim that reality is limited to what the five human senses can access is a baseless assumption. Why should it be the case that the scientifically accessible world is the sum total of all that is or can be known? One must step outside of science to make that kind of judgment, and that's a no-no by the very definition of scientism. Besides this, consider all that scientism rules out: things like good and evil, objective moral standards, human rights, and human value. Scientism, held consistently, is *very* expensive. It dispenses with concepts upon which human civilization depends for survival. For this reason, those who espouse scientism often do not apply it to other parts of their worldview. They are either oblivious to their own logical inconsistency, or they conveniently ignore the inevitable consequences of their own philosophy.

The key point to remember is that materialism and scientism are philosophical commitments brought to scientific discussions from the *outside*; they are not elements of science itself. Scientists investigate things like the laws of nature, physical mechanisms, and the history of the material world; their domain of inquiry—though its exact borders are notoriously fuzzy—does not actually restrict them from asking whether or not what they discover about nature is pointing *beyond* the material world to a higher reality. The scientist who concludes that it does is no less competent in his or her profession than the one who concludes that it does not. Yet the materialist and the advocate of scientism reject, from the get-go, even the *possibility* that scientific discoveries could imply the existence of anything that isn't empirically measurable (such as a transcendent Mind or the human soul). They insist that all data be interpreted according to the materialist philosophy. Evolutionary biologist Richard Lewontin admits this bias:

> It is not that the methods and institutions of science somehow compel us to accept a material explanation of the phenomenal world, but, on the contrary, that we are forced by our a priori adherence to material causes to create an apparatus of investigation and a set of concepts that produce material explanations, no matter how counterintuitive, no matter how mystifying to the uninitiated. Moreover, that materialism is absolute, for we cannot allow a Divine Foot in the door.[10]

Even if aspects of nature *seem* to be the product of a Mind, the scientist must stick to his or her materialist guns.

In addition to acknowledging how materialism is imposed upon science and not dictated by it, Lewontin makes an additional (but directly related) claim that deserves teasing out: that scientists should always seek natural causes to explain observed phenomena. This is a philosophical view known as *methodological naturalism*. On a certain level, methodological naturalism is uncontroversial. Of course we should seek natural explanations for what we observe in physics, chemistry, biology, and so on. If I wake up one morning to discover that mushrooms have sprung up on my lawn and I must know why, I shouldn't be open to the idea that invisible fungus fairies constructed them during the night. Rather, I should seek the natural cause for the mushrooms—spores and decaying organic matter. Similarly, when a scientist is trying to account for a new observation, he or she should operate on the assumption that there is an explanation that doesn't involve magic or God's miraculous intervention in nature. Most everyone would agree on this.

Significant conflict over methodological naturalism arises, however, when it is (over)extended to more fundamental questions, such as those concerned with the ultimate origin and nature of things. For example, consider this question: Why is the world rationally organized and thus intelligible to mankind? Scientific evidence shows us *that* the world is this way, but it cannot offer an explanation for it. Materialist proponents of methodological naturalism insist there must be a non-supernatural explanation (though we may not presently know it) for every question we can pose about nature, or else no explanation at all. By their lights, the idea that the world is orderly and comprehensible for no reason whatsoever is far preferable to proposing the existence of a Mind who made it so. (Notice how this attitude overlaps with scientism.)

In contrast, many nonmaterialists believe that while methodological naturalism is an important rule of thumb in scientific practice, evidence from fields such as cosmology and biology can legitimately be used to support philosophical arguments whose conclusions have theological significance. As a result, our knowledge of reality may be expanded well beyond the scope of scientific investigation. Therefore, we should be free to contemplate the possible philosophical and theistic implications of scientific discoveries without being wrongfully accused of having an antiscience mentality.

Some nonmaterialists, particularly those who are advocates of the Intelligent Design (ID) movement, hold that mindful design in nature can be detected *scientifically*, based upon (1) specific design markers in the structure of the universe and living systems, and (2) certain major explanatory failures of materialism. These proponents of ID argue that methodological naturalism can be reasonably suspended when the evidence strongly points to the involvement of intelligence in the natural order. They believe that scientists should be permitted to follow the evidence where it leads at the present rather than stringently excluding ID theory based upon a philosophical precommitment. Some nonmaterialists disagree; they are convinced that transcendent intelligence cannot be detected scientifically, though they still believe that nature is the result of God's handiwork.

In my view, the ID theorists make a good point: What *if* there are signs of intelligence in nature that can be detected through scientific investigation? If we rule out this possibility from the start, we are artificially limiting what nature is permitted to tell us one way or the other. It seems to me that we should be open-minded and willing to consider every tool at our disposal for finding out truths about the natural world. That said, this book will be concerned with science-supported philosophical arguments for the existence of a designing Mind in whose image we are made. Whatever one's view happens to be concerning how broadly to apply methodological naturalism in scientific research, it should be recognized that philosophy is not likewise restricted. Moreover, using evidence from the natural sciences to support philosophical argumentation in no way infringes upon the project of science itself.

> What *if* there are signs of intelligence in nature that can be detected through scientific investigation? If we rule out this possibility from the start, we are artificially limiting what nature is permitted to tell us.

It has been said that the business of science is taking things apart to see how they *work*, while the business of philosophy and theology is putting things together to see what they *mean*. When these methods of inquiry are allowed to come together, their synergistic partnership yields a far more complete and satisfying picture of the world than any of them can achieve alone.

The "God-of-the-Gaps" Objection

A common defense of the materialist approach to science is to say that positing the supernatural as an explanation for any aspect of nature commits the error known as *God-of-the-gaps*—plugging divine agency into current gaps in scientific knowledge. The argument typically goes as follows: As man's understanding of nature has grown, the space left for theistic explanations has been steadily shrinking. The areas presently unexplained—the deficiencies in scientific knowledge—are the spots where religious people tend to insert God rather than recognize a need for continued scientific exploration. The materialist may point to the various failed gaps arguments made throughout the history of science in an effort to show that rationality is gradually winning out over superstition—the category into which they place theological beliefs.

Admittedly, some theists have indeed made God-of-the-gaps claims that progress in the sciences eventually overturned. One example would be the now-discarded belief that God created every single variety of every single plant and animal species from scratch in an instantaneous act of supernatural creation. We now understand that there is a natural, observable explanation: Varieties of species arise through the spread and preservation of genetic mutations in populations of living organisms. Invoking God's *direct* agency to account for variations among species turned out to be a mistake.

Even so, the God-of-the-gaps label is often misused; it is not uncommon for materialists to unfairly apply it to philosophical conclusions that are based upon the *existing* evidence, not missing scientific information. For example, suggesting that a designing intelligence is responsible for the elegant mathematical order of the cosmos or the exquisite complexity of life is not a gaps argument; it is a philosophical conclusion drawn from mounds of data, not a lack thereof. In addition, there remain deep mysteries about the origin and character of nature which suggest *positive reasons* to suspect that a Mind was somehow involved (though not *necessarily* by way of miraculous intervention into the natural order). These situations are markedly different from gaps arguments because they involve an inference to the best explanation based upon the actual observations. This type of logical reasoning (known as *abductive reasoning*) is typical in science as well as detective work; though it does not yield certainty, it is quite useful in establishing the plausibility of a working hypothesis. Nevertheless, this is not to say that science should not continue to work toward closing holes in its account of nature, only that philosophical inferences about a designing Mind may very well be reasonable in light of the data and are by no means a hindrance to any further scientific research.

At the end of the day, even where scientific explanations of natural phenomena are relatively complete, the likelihood of a Maker is in no way diminished. This is not a zero-sum game. Theists fully recognize that God works through *primary* (direct) causation as well as *secondary* methods of causation, such as the laws and mechanisms he has built into nature. This understanding of divine agency in creation goes back at least as far as St. Augustine (354–430), who explained in his commentary on Genesis that God created the world with intrinsic potentialities that are realized over time through processes of growth and development. Whether something in the natural world is the product of primary or secondary causation, it is no less a product of the mind of the Maker.

As John Lennox puts it, insightful believers have no interest in a God of the gaps; they're arguing for the "God of the whole show": the God over what science has established, what it hasn't yet but might in the future, and everything that is, arguably, well outside its sphere of inquiry—the big *why* questions of cosmic existence, the rationality of nature, and the explanation for science itself.

The Essence of the Maker Thesis

One of the most common contemporary science-related objections to theism is, "There's not a shred of evidence for the existence of God." Granted, we are not able to prove (or disprove) God's existence scientifically, so instead of asking whether or not science *proves* God, the correct question to ask is whether or not his existence makes better sense of the available evidence. The overarching argument of this book—the Maker Thesis—is that certain discoveries of the natural sciences (1) support the inference that there is a Mind behind the universe with whom we share kinship, and (2) suggest that this Mind intended the success of the natural sciences. In other words, the origin and structure of nature, as well as the existence of the scientific enterprise itself, are best explained by a divine Maker who made us in his image and desired our awareness of him.

Instead of asking whether or not science *proves* God, the correct question to ask is whether or not his existence makes better sense of the available evidence.

I will argue for the Maker Thesis in three ways: (1) by using modern scientific evidence to support philosophical arguments for the existence of a Maker, (2) by explaining some of the many features of our universe and planetary home that had to converge for the investigation of nature to be possible, and (3) by demonstrating the necessity of a rational Mind and ensouled creatures to account for the effective practice of the natural sciences. We will explore a diversity of fields—physics, cosmology, earth science, philosophy of mind, neuroscience, and biochemistry—to make a cumulative case for the Maker Thesis, and end with a final discussion about how the Maker Thesis brings about a unified, smoothly integrated image of reality.

A good analogy for the grand cosmic coherence the Maker Thesis offers is one of those wooden peg puzzles small children often play with. Surely you've seen at least one in passing; the puzzle has a main wooden board with relief cutouts into which specific pieces will fit, and each of the corresponding pieces has a small peg attached to it so that it's easy to put in and take back out. Often the board itself is designed as a scene, such as a barnyard or a city block, and the pieces—animals or vehicles, in those cases—fit into their custom-shaped spots, completing the overall picture. Looking closely at the edges of the pieces, you can see hints to their visual context: maybe a sliver of green grass or blue sky, a segment of road lines or slice of sidewalk. In much the same way, the scientific and philosophical pieces that will be discussed in the following chapters fit snugly and coherently within the Maker Thesis framework (and therefore, within Christianity). Yet under materialism, we are left without a unifying frame and any satisfactory explanation for each of the separate pieces, even though their edges strongly suggest a common background picture.

A Historical Perspective on Natural Theology

The discipline concerned with making a case for the existence and nature of God using philosophical reasoning and observable reality is known as *natural theology*. One of the goals of natural theology is to demonstrate that, unlike theism, the materialist worldview is intrinsically deficient in terms of providing what scientist and theologian Alister McGrath describes as "a comprehensive and coherent interpretation of the natural order."[11] As mentioned earlier, the Maker Thesis seeks to provide what the materialist paradigm cannot. Thus, it is, properly speaking, an exercise in natural theology.

Natural theology's foundational idea—that the Maker of the world reveals himself to mankind through what he has made—has roots in very ancient theological writings. A hallmark example is found in one of the psalms of King David (c. 1000 BC):

> The heavens declare the glory of God,
>   and the sky above proclaims his handiwork.
> Day to day pours out speech,
>   and night to night reveals knowledge.
> There is no speech, nor are there words,
>   whose voice is not heard.
> Their voice goes out through all the earth,
>   and their words to the end of the world (Psalm 19:1-4).

Notice the psalmist's use of linguistic metaphors—"speech," "voice," "words"—to describe the universal message of creation. In beholding the beautiful and orderly skies, both day and night, we glean knowledge of the existence of their Creator. This passage from the Psalms poetically describes how nature speaks to mankind's aesthetic sense and theological intuition. More than a millennium later, the apostle Paul went so far as to say that God is so evident in the natural order that those who do not acknowledge him are without excuse (Romans 1:20).

The historical roots of natural theology are fascinating, and they are intertwined with the central claims of the Maker Thesis in important, and sometimes surprising, ways. For this reason, several chapters of this book are devoted to an overview of the philosophers, theologians, and scientists who have significantly impacted the science and theology conversation over the past two-and-a-half millennia. These chapters will demonstrate the rich scholarly pedigree of the claims included in the Maker Thesis while sketching out some basics of the related scientific progress. If you aren't exactly a history buff, have no fear! These fast-paced historical survey chapters will be intermingled with chapters that cover the contemporary scientific topics relevant to the Maker Thesis, so you won't have to digest all the history at once. My not-so-secret hope is that you will gain a deeper appreciation for the relevance of intellectual history in contemporary discussions about these big ideas.

Which View of Creation?

Many books that discuss the intersection of science and theology do so from a particular perspective on how the Genesis creation narrative should be interpreted. Thus, they take specific views on things like the age of the earth and whether or not biological history included universal common descent (the evolutionary descent of all species from a primordial ancestor). The Maker Thesis transcends those kinds of discussions and instead focuses the attention on a higher essential: the existence of a Creator of all things in whose image man is fashioned.

The key advantage of this approach is that it sidesteps what have, unfortunately, become emotionally poisoned secondary issues and makes finding initial common ground with a science-oriented skeptic much easier. "Mere creation"—with its echo of C.S. Lewis's ecumenical "mere Christian" philosophy of evangelism—is an appropriate way to think of the Maker Thesis strategy. Note that mere creation, as I am defining it, goes beyond basic theism in that it includes the claim that human beings occupy a special place in the creation because of their unique relationship to the Maker.

In my experience dialoguing with skeptics, a mere creation approach facilitates more open and productive conversations that are less likely to end in a stalemate over the minutia of evolutionary theory or scientific dating methods. It allows us to take the discussion to a different plane and get to the real crux of the matter—what the objective evidence, paired with sound reasoning, implies about the existence of a Maker and about human nature. In many instances, the answer to this question represents the threshold between all-out skepticism about Christian theism and intellectual openness to its other central doctrines. The Maker Thesis is not a complete apologetic; it is a stepping-stone, but an essential one. After all, no one is going to be persuaded of John 1:14 (the Word was made flesh) if they are not first persuaded of John 1:3 (there is a creating Word). My sincere hope is that no matter where you fall on the creation views spectrum, you will be encouraged and better equipped to impact the kingdom for the glory of God as a result of reading this book.

As Christians working to fulfill the Great Commission in a scientific age, we cannot afford to simply ignore the natural sciences. I'm reminded of a statement made by the Swiss theologian Emil Brunner, who wrote that we must do what we can to remove "the obstacles which lie on the road between the gospel and its audience—namely, those obstacles which are amenable to intellectual reflection."[12] When we invest the time and mental energy to educate ourselves on some of the foundational issues involved, we become better able to remove common science-related roadblocks from the path of the seeker and offer good reasons to believe that there is a Maker in whose image we are made.

Shall we begin?

Chapter 2

The Divine in Nature:
A Big (and Ancient) Idea

The moon's bright globe, the sun and stars are nurtured
By a spirit in them. Mind infuses each part
And animates the universe's whole mass.[1]

Vergil

What can be so obvious and clear, as we gaze
up at the sky and observe the heavenly bodies,
as that there is some divine power of surpassing
intelligence by which they are ordered?[2]

Cicero

One major facet of the Maker Thesis, the claim that there is a transcendent Mind in whose image mankind is created, has roots that predate Christianity by centuries and the rise of modern science by millennia. In the earliest philosophical literature of the Western tradition, great thinkers discussed the beauty and regularities of nature as being manifestations of a divine rationality that transcends or pervades the cosmos. These ancient philosophers believed that the human mind is somehow connected to this ordering intellect or principle—that man's rationality is a spark of the divine. As we survey some of these great thinkers, we will trace the development of ideas that are central to the Maker Thesis.

Philosopher and mathematician Pythagoras of Samos (c. 570–495 BC), the very thinker traditionally credited with inventing the term "philosophy" (*philo* = love, *sophia* = wisdom), left behind no writings, but many of his alleged teachings are recorded in early biographies or referenced by other ancient writers. Unfortunately, the majority of relevant surviving historical documents are dated centuries after Pythagoras, so there is scholarly debate about whether or not later "Pythagorean" philosophers had an accurate understanding of his teachings. In any case, those of the Pythagorean School believed that number is itself a divinity that underlies all of physical reality, a pervasive "world soul" of which human souls are fragments.[3] The Pythagoreans saw the orderliness of the world as something deep and all-encompassing, with mystical interconnections between number, mind, and the material world.

Pythagoreanism influenced later Greek philosophy, particularly through the work of Plato (c. 429–347 BC). Plato agreed that number is related to the organization of the visible cosmos, but for him, this was not the result of number being the essence of material existence. Instead, he believed that the physical world is composed of imperfect copies of immaterial, transcendent "Forms." This idea is artfully illustrated in Plato's *Timaeus* dialogue, which includes an elaborate account of the creation of the cosmos. Timaeus, a Pythagorean character, maintains that the beauty, regularities, and intelligibility of nature are explained by a benevolent craftsman who brought order out of formlessness and purposively framed the universe according to the eternal, mathematical Forms. He says that the world was "crafted in reference to that which is grasped by reason," meaning the abstract perfections the human mind can arrive upon when reasoning from what is visible to us.[4] For example, when we encounter a spherical object, we can reason to the abstract idea of a perfect sphere, which exists only in the realm of Forms. Timaeus goes on to explain that "God invented and gave us sight to the end that we might behold the courses of intelligence in the heaven, and apply them to the courses of our own intelligence which are akin to them."[5] Through the words of Timaeus, Plato draws a connection between the rationality of nature and the powers of the human mind.

In *The Republic*, Plato argues that philosophical insights about higher reality (the Forms) result from the contemplation of nature. He says, "The spangled heavens should be used as a pattern and with a view to that higher knowledge."[6] However, he goes beyond discussion of the Forms to comment upon natural revelation of the divine when he remarks that the true astronomer will see that the heavenly bodies "are framed by the Creator of them in the most perfect manner."[7] The point is that an agent is deemed responsible for the creation of the visible world. The Forms themselves lack such power; they are just patterns. Plato believed that there are characteristics of the natural world that draw the human mind upward to a transcendent reality. Granted, there is debate over whether Plato truly believed in the existence of a *personal* craftsman or he was simply using personification to describe a more panentheistic view of the universe. For our purposes, the interpretation is not all that important, since, either way, we can understand Plato as saying that there is divine creative intelligence reflected in both the material world and the human intellect.

A few centuries later, aspects of Platonism became integrated with Jewish thought about God, the orderliness of nature, and man's ability to detect that orderliness. An excellent example of this is the work of Philo Judaeus (c. 20 BC–AD 50), an Alexandrian Jew and Middle Platonist who has been hailed as "one of the most remarkable literary phenomena of the Hellenistic world."[8] Philo recognized the rational organization of the visible world, and, like Plato, believed that it was created according to a preconceived plan, much like a building is constructed based upon an architect's blueprints. However, a major difference in Philo's thinking was that he believed this cosmic plan was not some self-existent entity; instead, he saw it as being situated in—and dependent upon—the mind of God:

As therefore the city, when previously shadowed out in

the mind of the man of architectural skill had no external place, but was stamped solely in the mind of the workman, so in the same manner neither can the world which existed in ideas have had any other local position except the divine reason which made them...[9]

Philo argued that the "idea of ideas, the Reason of God," what he calls the *Logos* ("word" or "reason"), pervades nature, accounting for its physical structure as well as man's faculty of reason. Significantly, he related this to the Jewish doctrine of mankind being made in the image of God.[10] In other words, because God's intellect is reflected, to a finite extent, in his image-bearers, we are naturally inclined to detect signs of the Maker in his workmanship. Perhaps Philo saw the remarkable compatibility between the Greek concept of *Logos* and the Hebrew notion of the creative "word" of God, which we find in passages such as Psalm 33:6: "By the word of the LORD the heavens were made, and by the breath of his mouth all their host," and realized how well Hellenistic philosophy could support and illuminate Scripture.

> Because God's intellect is reflected, to a finite extent, in his image-bearers, we are naturally inclined to detect signs of the Maker in his workmanship.

Philo was not the first philosopher to situate the Platonic Forms in the mind of God. Antiochus of Ascalon (c. 130–69 BC), another Middle Platonist, called them "the thoughts of God," and it is considered possible (though not provable) that he adopted this thinking from philosophers who were educated at Plato's famous Academy.[11] Nevertheless, it was Philo's writings that went on to influence the early Christian theologians who identified Philo's *Logos* with the *Logos* in the apostle John's writings—Jesus Christ, the eternal Word through whom all things were made (John 1:1-3).[12]

Another fascinating work that synthesizes elements of Greek and

Jewish thought is *Wisdom of Solomon,* a book of Jewish wisdom literature typically dated within the first century BC or first century AD. *Wisdom* contains intriguing passages about God's mathematically ordered creation; the (unknown) writer says that God "ordered all things by measure and number and weight."[13] It is quite interesting that a book whose major theme is God-given wisdom would use language associated with mathematics to describe the structure of creation. *Wisdom* explicitly affirms the legitimacy of seeing the natural world as a revelation of the divine and condemns those who study nature yet do not recognize its Maker:

> Yes, naturally stupid are all who are unaware of God, and who, from good things seen, have not been able to discover Him-who-is, or, by studying the works, have not recognized the Artificer...since through the grandeur and beauty of the creatures we may, by analogy, contemplate their Author...they have no excuse: if they are capable of acquiring enough knowledge to be able to investigate the world, how have they been so slow to find its Master?[14]

What a striking resemblance there is between these words and those found in the aforementioned passage from Romans, where the apostle Paul writes, "For his invisible attributes, namely, his eternal power and divine nature, have been clearly perceived, ever since the creation of the world, in the things that have been made. So they are without excuse" (Romans 1:20). It is not much of a stretch to suppose that Paul, a highly educated Jew and citizen of Rome, was familiar with Hellenistic Jewish literature such as *Wisdom*; perhaps it influenced the phrasing he used in his epistle.

The idea of a rational Creator with whom man has a unique kinship continued in non-Jewish writings as well. A Roman philosopher and mathematician known as Nicomachus of Gerasa (c. 60–120) was an important member of a first-century AD revival of Pythagorean thought known as *Neo-Pythagoreanism.* He was quite famous and was considered by some to be a link in the so-called "golden chain" of true philosophers.[15] Nicomachus's philosophy of nature reflects the Platonic view that the material world is modeled upon a mathematical plan, but places that plan in the divine intellect. In chapter IV of his highly successful *Introduction to Arithmetic*, Nicomachus said that arithmetic is the foundational form of all mathematics, that it "existed before all the others in the mind of the creating God like some universal and exemplary plan, relying upon which, as a design and archetypal example, the creator of the universe sets in order his material creations."[16] In chapter VI he went on to say:

> All that has by nature with systematic method been arranged in the universe seems both in part and as a whole to have been determined and ordered in accordance with number, by the forethought and the mind of him that created all things; for the pattern was fixed, like a preliminary sketch, by the domination of number preexistent in the mind of the world-creating God...so that with reference to it, as to an artistic plan, should be created all these things, time, motion, the heavens, the stars, all sorts of revolutions.[17]

Though he does not explicitly say that the mathematical orderliness of nature is a *revelation* of the divine, his words seem to suggest it. It is remarkable that we see such similarity between Nicomachus's philosophy and Philo's; though one was pagan and one was Jewish, both placed the cosmic plan in the mind of the Creator rather than a Platonic realm of eternal Forms.

Early Christian Thought on Natural Revelation

In the first few centuries after Christ, the early patristic period of church history, an interesting metaphor for the way nature communicates truths about God began to appear in theological writings. Several of the church fathers spoke of creation as a "book" that, along with

Holy Scripture, serves as a vehicle of divine revelation. They taught that the awe-inspiring harmony and beauty of the world disclose the transcendent wisdom and power of the Maker behind it all, and that observing nature's wonders is like reading words on a page.

It is not entirely clear who first used the "book of nature" metaphor. St. Anthony the Abbot (251–356), one of the Egyptian desert fathers and a founder of Christian monasticism, remarked, "My book…is the nature of things that are made, and it is present whenever I wish to read the words of God."[18] Subtle suggestions of the metaphor also appear in the works of several other fourth-century church fathers. St. Athanasius (297–373), Bishop of Alexandria, wrote that "the creatures are like letters proclaiming in loud voices to their Divine Master and Creator the harmony and order of things."[19] In a remarkable passage, he draws a parallel between the Word of John's Gospel—the *Logos* through whom all things were made—and words of human language:

> By the greatness and the beauty of the creatures proportionately the Maker of them is seen. For just as by looking up to the heaven and seeing its order and the light of the stars, it is possible to infer the Word Who ordered these things…for if when a word proceeds from men we infer that the mind is its source, and by thinking about the word, see with our reason the mind which it reveals, by far greater evidence and incomparably more, seeing the power of the Word, we receive knowledge also of His good Father.[20]

Athanasius is arguing that nature points to the mind of the Creator in a way that is analogous to how human language is indicative of mind. Just as we can rightfully ascribe instances of spoken or written language to a rational source, we can attribute the regularities and splendor of nature to its Maker.

A contemporary of Athanasius, St. Basil, Bishop of Caesarea (330–379), taught that human rationality is part of the image of God in which we are made and that our intellectual capabilities allow us to grasp the language of God's natural revelation:

> We were made in the image and likeness of our Creator, endowed with intellect and reason, so that our nature was complete and we could know God. In this way, continuously contemplating the beauty of creatures, through them as if they were letters and words, we could read God's wisdom and providence over all things.[21]

Like Athanasius, Basil does not explicitly mention the "book" of nature, but we see allusions to the metaphor when he refers to created things as letters and words by which we may glean knowledge of God. He saw a resonance between the human mind and the material manifestations of the Creator's.

The book of nature can be read even by the illiterate, so all men have access to some knowledge of the divine.

Perhaps the best-known early reference to the book of nature is found in the *Sermons* of St. Augustine (354–430), Bishop of Hippo and the most influential of the Western church fathers. He called the spectacle of creation "a great book" that we must attend to; he said, "Look carefully at it top and bottom, observe it, read it. God did not write in letters with ink but he placed what is created itself in front of you to recognize him in; he set before your eyes all these things he has made. Why look for a louder voice? Heaven and earth cries out to you: God made me."[22] Truly, he asks, could the Creator be any more obvious in revealing himself to mankind? Unlike the text of Scripture, the book of nature can be read even by the illiterate, so all men have access to some knowledge of the divine. Creation conveys this truth to us through our observations and rationality just as words on a page convey ideas to a reader.

The Book of Nature Metaphor: Science and Poetry Converge

The book of nature metaphor has endured quite well down through the centuries in part because of its use in fine poetry. Here's one example of particular interest because of its direct connection to both a great poet and an eminent man of science. In May of 1857, the fiftieth birthday of Harvard biologist and geologist Louis Agassiz was celebrated in Cambridge, Massachusetts. To mark the occasion, Henry Wadsworth Longfellow composed a poem in honor of his dear friend. The verses beautifully reflect Agassiz's conviction that nature, like written Scripture, is part of God's revelation to mankind:

> And Nature, the old nurse, took
>   The child upon her knee,
> Saying: "Here is a story-book
>   Thy Father has written for thee."
>
> "Come, wander with me," she said,
>   "Into regions yet untrod;
> And read what is still unread
>   In the manuscripts of God."
>
> And he wandered away and away
>   With Nature, the dear old nurse,
> Who sang to him night and day
>   The rhymes of the universe.
>
> And whenever the way seemed long,
>   Or his heart began to fail,
> She would sing a more wonderful song,
>   Or tell a more marvellous tale.[23]

Augustine was well educated in ancient Greek philosophy and, like

Philo, reframed the Platonic doctrine of the Forms—in this case, for Christian theology. No one would dare to say that God didn't have a rational plan for his creation, Augustine argues; but this plan "must be thought to exist nowhere but in the very mind of the Creator."[24] He goes on to declare it sacrilege to believe that God used a self-existent model for the world, because that would mean something independent of God could be co-eternal with him. This idea goes against the orthodox Christian doctrine of God as the only timeless, uncreated being.

In his commentary on Genesis, Augustine echoes the *Wisdom of Solomon* when he mentions measure, number, and weight "in which, as it is written, God has arranged all things," and then asks whether these numerical concepts were themselves created or existed prior to the material world.[25] His conclusion is that there was nothing outside of God before the original act of creation, and therefore the immaterial mathematical design must have existed "in him" as ideas.[26] As for humanity's discernment of the orderliness of the physical world, Augustine explains that the soul of man is illumined by God in a manner that enables us to detect the rationality of creation.[27] It is because we are made in the image of the Maker himself that we are cognizant of his natural self-revelation.

During the medieval period, Christian scholars worked tirelessly to preserve and transmit the learning of the classical tradition.[28] The book of nature metaphor for God's natural revelation flourished, though it underwent a few subtle developments. A monk from Constantinople, St. Maximus the Confessor (580–662), wrote: "The natural law, as if it were a book, holds and sustains the harmony of the whole of the universe. Material bodies are like the book's characters and syllables...but allow only a partial knowledge."[29] We see that Maximus placed great value upon natural revelation while cautioning that it is deficient without the superior revelation found in Scripture. He believed that nature's message is limited in that it can only impart knowledge of the existence and wisdom of the *Logos*; it can give evidence for a transcendent

Creator, but not the necessary specifics of Christian doctrine. But this was not to devalue natural revelation. On the contrary, he said that "it is gathering with reverence all these different manifestations of his, that we are led toward a unique and coherent representation of the truth, and [God] makes himself known to us as the Creator, by analogy from the visible, created world."[30] Maximus maintained that natural and special revelation work together in harmony to convey knowledge of God.

By the twelfth century, Plato's *Timaeus* was central to the curriculum of natural philosophy (roughly speaking, the study of nature) in the universities, so it is not surprising that great emphasis was placed upon the mathematical rationality in nature. The human intellect was considered part of the natural order and thus instinctively in tune with it. For this reason, man's mind was regarded as the perfect instrument for the study of the universe.[31] In *The Metalogicon* of John of Salisbury (c. 1120–1180), Bishop of Chartres, we see the ongoing interaction with Platonism in Christian thinking about the orderliness of the natural world. John critiqued the doctrine of the self-existent, eternal Platonic Forms, saying that they (if they exist) must have come from "him by Whom all things have been made."[32] He stressed that all truths, including mathematical ones, depend upon the mind of God for their existence and truthfulness. He echoed Philo, *Wisdom of Solomon*, and Augustine when he said that "God is number innumerable, weight incalculable, and measure inestimable. And in Him alone all things that have been made in number, in 'weight,' and in measure, have been created."[33] About the intellectual abilities that distinguish mankind from all other creatures, John said, "For God, breathing life into man, willed that he partake of the divine reason."[34] Thus we see two key ideas in these passages from *The Metalogicon*: The rationally ordered world is intelligible only to God's image-bearers, and these image-bearers are meant to contemplate its meaning.

A few centuries later, Raymond of Sebond (1385–1436), a doctor of both medicine and theology at Toulouse, penned a work entitled *Natural Theology*, in which he wrote, "Every creature is nothing but a word, written by God's finger; like many different words, all these creatures compose one book which is called the book of creatures."[35] Significantly, he emphasized the fact that human beings are "the most important word contained therein."[36] Raymond believed that we need both natural and special revelation and that these two books will never contradict one another. Like other great thinkers before him, he saw the book of nature as something man has an innate capacity to comprehend, and considered it to be an interpretive tool for the words of Scripture.[37] His point about the universal accessibility of natural revelation was particularly appropriate in his day, since Scripture had not yet been translated into the common language of the people. Nature was something open before the eyes of all.

As we shall see later on, the writings of these ancient and medieval philosophers and theologians went on to have a noticeable influence on the brilliant natural philosophers responsible for the rise of what we now call modern science.

Key Points

- The concept of natural revelation—a divine Creator revealing himself through nature—is found in some of the oldest theological and philosophical writings of Western civilization, including ancient Greek philosophy and the Old and New Testaments.

- The Platonic ideas of nature being constructed based upon a rational plan, that the contemplation of the material world draws the mind upward toward belief in a Creator, and that the human intellect is somehow akin to that transcendent Mind, were found by early Jewish and Christian theologians to be helpful in speaking about the existence and rationality of God and about man being made in God's image.

- Some church fathers discussed God's natural revelation using the metaphor of a book in which created things are letters and words communicating his message to us. The material creation came to be seen as one of the two books of God's divine revelation.

- Through the end of the medieval period, a major theme of both natural philosophy and natural theology was the mathematical orderliness of the cosmos and the fitness of the human intellect for grasping it.

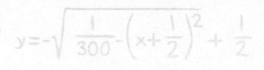

Chapter 3

The Origin and Structure of the Cosmos: Finite and Finely Tuned

The details differ, but the essential elements in the
astronomical and biblical accounts of Genesis
are the same: the chain of events leading to man
commenced suddenly and sharply at a definite
moment in time, in a flash of light and energy.[1]

Robert Jastrow

Astronomy leads us to a unique event, a universe
which was created out of nothing, one with the
very delicate balance needed to provide exactly the
conditions required to permit life, and one which has
an underlying (one might say "supernatural") plan.[2]

Arno Penzias

I remember the dramatic paradigm shift I experienced when I first realized that the world didn't begin turning the moment I was born. I must have been around four or five years old the day I pointed to a photo taken of my parents and grandparents while they were on a vacation together and asked, "But where am I?" The answer was that I had not yet been born, and I then had to come to grips with the fact that there were events that predated my own existence. I soon came to understand that the same was true for my parents and my grandparents, my great-grandparents, and back, and back, and back throughout all of human history...but this didn't change the strangeness of the thought that I had a *beginning*.

It still feels quite odd to ponder the fact that I've not always existed, but what I think is far more mind-boggling is the idea of an absolute *cosmic* origin. We have an adequate scientific explanation for how each of us came to be at a certain point in time, how biological reproduction works—human beings arise from other human beings going back through countless generations. But when it comes to the beginning of the universe itself, we're left with a major conundrum. Our best science indicates that all the material building blocks of the world and space-time itself had a beginning. How do we wrap our minds around the concept of the universe springing into existence from utter *nothingness*—a state in which there was no matter, space, or time? What could have caused this to happen?

The finitude of the universe is only the beginning (pun not intended) of the scientific enigma. Extensive cosmological data also suggest that the cosmos is extraordinarily fine-tuned for the existence of complex life—or any life at all for that matter. On paper, minuscule alterations in many of the physical parameters built into the fabric of physical reality yield theoretical universes in which stars, planets, and even the chemistry necessary for living organisms to emerge would be impossible. Yet against inconceivable odds, all the necessary constraints align in just the right way. This state of affairs is known in cosmology as the fine-tuning problem.

This chapter will explore the scientific evidence for the cosmic origin event and for the fine-tuning required for the existence of life. What we will see is that our best data from physics and cosmology support philosophical arguments for a transcendent, mindful cause of the universe. In perfect accord with the Maker Thesis, it appears as if the universe is the brainchild of a cosmic mastermind who has specifically orchestrated the many interconnected details of this grand, life-permitting scheme.

The Inevitability of a Cosmic Beginning

Early twentieth-century theoretical physics and astrophysics brought about a paradigm shift in our understanding of the cosmos. In the 1920s, a Belgian priest, astronomer, and cosmologist by the name of Georges Lemaître devised a solution to the equations of Albert Einstein's theory of general relativity that suggested a universe in a state of expansion (a solution that had been calculated independently by Russian physicist Alexander Friedmann). Over the next few years, Lemaître further developed the model, which posited a universe exploding out of an original "primeval atom" (what later came to be known as *big bang theory*). When he spoke personally with Einstein about the concept of cosmic evolution from this primeval atom, Einstein's response was, "No, not that, that suggests too much the creation."[3] Einstein vastly preferred an eternally stable universe that needed no higher explanation for its existence, but he was forced to relinquish this idea when, in 1929, American astronomer Edwin Hubble's telescopic observations at the Mount Wilson Observatory provided convincing empirical support for the Friedmann-Lemaître model. Hubble's work confirmed that other galaxies are racing away from our Milky Way in every direction rather than remaining immobile, and this indicated that the universe itself is expanding. As Einstein had remarked to Lemaître, this indeed pointed to a cosmic beginning.

Einstein's Little Lamb

Though one of the most brilliant physicists in history, Albert Einstein was not immune to allowing philosophical bias to influence his science. When his theory of relativity seemed to indicate that the universe is not static (in a fixed state, unchanging in size), he introduced a mathematical factor into his equations to offset what he considered an unacceptable implication of the theory. This "cosmological constant" is represented in the equations by the Greek letter *lambda* (λ), and came to be whimsically referred to as "Einstein's little lamb"—and everywhere that Einstein went, the lamb was sure to go. It is said that Einstein called his cosmological constant the "biggest blunder" of his career, since he could have been the one to predict cosmic expansion had he not manipulated his equations in order to avoid it. Much later, in the 1990s, a modified version of the cosmological constant was reintroduced to account for the acceleration of cosmic expansion.

To understand why an expanding universe must have had a definitive beginning, consider the following. No matter which direction into space astronomers point their high-powered telescopes, distant galaxies are flying outward at a high rate of speed. This doesn't mean that our galaxy is the center from which all else is rushing away; if we inhabited a planet in any other galaxy, astronomers would observe this very same phenomenon because it is the expansion of *space itself* that causes this apparent recession of everything from the location of any observer.

To get a better handle on this nonintuitive idea, think of space-time as the surface of an expanding sphere embedded with galaxies and galaxy clusters. Notice how this geometry eliminates the concept of the universe having any center at all, because it's nonsensical to ask where the center is on the surface of a spherical object. As the surface of the sphere expands (the "inside" of the sphere is totally irrelevant), the galaxies and galaxy clusters get further and further away from each other. Now if we imagine this process in reverse, extrapolating backward in time, the sphere would shrink and all these galaxies would get closer and closer together. We should reason that this cannot have been going on for an infinite amount of time. Indeed, today's standard model of cosmology—or big bang theory—says that there must have been a first moment at which all matter, energy, and *space-time itself* suddenly emerged from an infinitely hot and infinitely dense point, a moment cosmologists call the space-time singularity. Prior to this singularity, there was nothing, not even time, which is virtually impossible for temporal creatures to imagine.

Not surprisingly, many nontheists have found the standard model repugnant, typically because cosmic emergence from nothing smacks of divine creation. In fact, the astronomer who facetiously coined the phrase "big bang," Sir Fred Hoyle (1915–2001), rejected the theory because of the fact that it "openly invites the concept of creation."[4] Even as late as 1959, the majority of physicists and astronomers in America refused to believe that the universe did not have an infinite age.[5] The past half-century has witnessed a string of alternative theories, some of which included an ultimate beginning, and some that did not. It is striking that the models that have posited a past-eternal universe have turned out, time and time again, to be unworkable in terms of the theoretical physics involved.

Robert Jastrow: Scientist and Conflicted Agnostic

Robert Jastrow, physicist and founding director of NASA's Goddard Institute for Space Studies, gained popularity in the second half of the twentieth century through his science writing and numerous television appearances. He was appreciated for his ability to speak on topics such as astronomy, earth science, and the space program in a manner accessible to the general public. Although he was an agnostic, Jastrow was sometimes quite candid about the theistic implications of modern physics and cosmology. In one television interview, after explaining the scientific data for a finite universe, he concluded:

> So there's a beginning. There's a point in time from which it all started, and that's a remarkable thing; it has a very strong theological flavor to it, and that intrigued me because I am an agnostic. If there was a beginning, a moment of creation of the universe, then there was a Creator. And a Creator is not compatible with agnosticism.[6]

In his 1978 book, *God and the Astronomers*, Jastrow remarked,

Theologians generally are delighted with the proof that the Universe had a beginning, but astronomers are curiously upset. Their reactions provide an interesting demonstration of the response of the scientific mind—supposedly a very objective mind—when evidence uncovered by science itself leads to a conflict with the articles of faith in our profession. [7]

Later, in a 1982 interview with *Christianity Today* magazine, he spoke even more boldly:

Astronomers now find they have painted themselves into a corner because they have proven, by their own methods, that the world began abruptly in an act of creation...And they have found that all this happened as a product of forces they cannot hope to discover. That there are what I or anyone would call supernatural forces at work is now, I think, a scientifically proven fact. [8]

In 2003, a landmark theorem constructed by Arvind Borde, Alan Guth, and Alexander Vilenkin indicated that any universe that has been expanding throughout its history must have had a beginning. [9] Granted, as we look back in time to the first microsecond of the universe's existence (think of it as rolling the film of cosmic history in reverse), the laws of nature themselves break down; that tiny fraction of a second after the singularity, known as *Planck time* (named after physicist Max Planck), is entirely opaque, even to our best science. I've heard the situation described as a drawn window shade beyond which we will never see, despite any future advancements in astrophysics. But even with this being the case, the Borde-Guth-Vilenkin theorem (hereafter, BGV theorem) still holds; to put it very simply, no matter what physical conditions existed during Planck time, a beginning remains inescapable.

More recently, in a 2015 essay entitled "The Beginning of the

Universe," Vilenkin (an agnostic) openly acknowledged that if the big bang represents the true beginning of the universe, disquieting questions arise: "A beginning in what? Caused by what? And determined by what or whom? These questions have prompted physicists to make every attempt to avoid a cosmic beginning."[10] The conclusion of his essay is remarkable:

> The answer to the question, "Did the universe have a beginning?" is, "It probably did." We have no viable models of an eternal universe. The BGV theorem gives us reason to believe that such models simply cannot be constructed. When physicists or theologians ask me about the BGV theorem, I am happy to oblige. But my own view is that the theorem does not tell us anything about the existence of God. A deep mystery remains. The laws of physics that describe the quantum creation of the universe also describe its evolution. This seems to suggest that they have some independent existence. What exactly this means, we don't know. And why are these laws the ones we have? Why not other laws? We have no way to begin to address this mystery.[11]

According to Vilenkin, it's not just that there is currently no workable theory that allows for a past-eternal universe; we have good reason to believe that a no-beginning model is impossible. Also significant is his implicit admission that science cannot address the metaphysical questions that arise when we contemplate an ultimate beginning. Moreover, he acknowledges the fact that the mathematical laws describing our universe seem to have "some independent existence," that the laws of physics were a reality *before* they had anything whatsoever to describe. When Vilenkin says that we "have no way to begin to address" these questions, the idea is not that science hasn't *yet* been able to answer them; it is that such questions fall outside the scope of science.

Ultimately, Vilenkin seems to be content with permanent mystery rather than exploring how philosophy and theology might enrich our understanding of reality. When he says that the BGV theorem doesn't say anything about the existence of God, he glosses over the fact that a beginning of anything—universes included—necessitates a cause for that beginning.

The Philosophers Got There First

Although the scientific evidence for a finite universe is stronger than ever, many materialists argue that we simply cannot know what triggered the big bang, and that saying God was the cause commits the god-of-the-gaps mistake—using the concept of divine agency to fill in a gap in our scientific knowledge rather than working to uncover a fully naturalistic explanation. This is not the case. When we consider the cosmic origin from a philosophical perspective, we see that an immaterial, timeless, uncaused agent is actually the most (I would argue the *only*) reasonable option.

The debate over whether or not physical reality had an ultimate beginning goes back thousands of years; the idea of an eternal universe is deeply rooted in ancient Greek philosophy. We've already seen that Plato offered a creation account in which a craftsman fashioned the cosmos, but this "creation" involved reshaping and organizing preexistent material that had been lying about in a chaotic heap from eternity. Aristotle, a disciple of Plato, actually saw eternality as one of the perfections of the cosmos, yet did not see God as unnecessary for explaining the world. He believed that the universe is eternally caused by God, the "unmoved mover." In his book *On the Heavens*, Aristotle said that "the heaven as a whole neither came into being nor admits of destruction, as some assert, but is one and eternal, with no end or beginning of its total duration, containing and embracing in itself the infinity of time."[12]

> When we consider the cosmic origin from a philosophical perspective, we see that an immaterial, timeless, uncaused agent is actually the most reasonable option.

More than a thousand years later, a Muslim philosopher and theologian known as Al-Ghazali (c. 1055–1111), who studied the teachings of the Greek philosophers, challenged the notion of an eternal world. After observing that some Muslim thinkers of his time were being influenced by Greek ideas and were thus denying God's original creation of all things, he set to work explaining why the concept of a past-infinite universe involves logical absurdities.[13] Al-Ghazali made two arguments to this effect. First, he pointed out that if the universe has an infinite past, this would mean there has been an infinite series of past events, one after another, leading up to the present. Suppose we could label today as "Event 0," yesterday as "Event – 1," the day before yesterday as "Event – 2," and so on. If the universe is eternal, that would mean we could, in theory, count backward forever, never reaching a first cosmic event. Al-Ghazali realized that this conception of the world's history is impossible because an *actual infinity* of past events cannot be passed through, one at a time, to arrive at the present. A definite starting point is necessary.

A helpful analogy is a series of dominoes which need to fall, one after the other, until the final domino, "Event 0," falls down. If the line of preceding dominoes is infinite, "Event 0" (which represents present day) would never be attained. Just as you cannot pass through an infinite series of falling dominoes, you cannot count down the events of cosmic history over an eternal past with any hope of reaching the present.[14] However, if you have a finite past with a beginning—a very first domino that topples over—then it *is* possible to get to this moment in time. Note that the line of falling dominoes could start at a finite point—"Event 1"—and go on forever by adding one domino after another, just like one could start counting with number one and count forward without ever reaching an end. This is what we call a *potential infinity*, which, unlike an actual infinity, is unproblematic.

Second, Al-Ghazali argued that the idea of an infinite collection of things—which an eternal series of past events would be—cannot exist in reality. An infinite number of something would be a *complete collection*; to say it is increasing moment by moment would be nonsensical because you cannot *add* to an already infinite number of things.

A simple thought experiment helps to drive home this point. Imagine you are a poultry farmer with a prolific flock of chickens. In fact, you currently have an infinite number of chickens. Now imagine that every one of your chickens lays a fertile egg, and every egg hatches. How many chickens would you then have? You already had an infinite collection of birds; there's no such thing as *double* infinity. What if you then slaughtered all the adult chickens for the local neighborhood chicken stew cook-off? How many chickens would you have then? It would make no sense to say that you have half the number you once had but that you still have an infinite number of chickens. This is an example of what is meant by a concept that results in logical absurdities. As with the domino example, a *potential* infinite is no problem for your chicken farm. You could begin with one hen and one rooster and move toward an infinite number of chickens over time. They could reproduce forever into the future, though you would never arrive at a complete, infinite set of chickens.

From the impossibility of having an infinite collection of events, it follows that the universe must be finite in age. It had to have had an absolute beginning upon which physical events began happening throughout a progression of time. Some have tried to avoid this problem by proposing that our universe is just one member of an enormous cosmic landscape of universes popping into existence, each with its own finite timeline, but this does not escape Al-Ghazali's point. A multiverse would still need to have an ultimate origin, since each cosmic birth event would, theoretically, be one in a series of events which could not have been occurring, one after another, from eternity past. We'd never get to our big bang event because an infinite series of other events would have to have occurred first, and it would be impossible to pass through them all. Moreover, the BGV theorem, which says that any viable cosmic model must have a beginning, also applies to an expanding multiverse model. This means that an eternal multiverse is not only logically problematic, it also appears to be scientifically unfeasible.

The only reasonable conclusion, given both the scientific evidence and philosophical restraints, is that all of physical reality—space-time, matter, and energy—had a beginning. At some point in the finite past, there was an ultimate origin event, what philosophers and theologians refer to as *creatio ex nihilo*—a Latin phrase that means "creation out of nothing."

The philosopher and theologian who has expended an enormous amount of effort toward further developing Al-Ghazali's work, William Lane Craig, refers to his version as the *kalam* cosmological argument for the existence of God. *Kalam* is an Arabic word that refers to medieval Islamic theology, and it is quite fitting given the major contribution of Al-Ghazali, though it should be noted that the argument has roots that go back at least as far as a Christian philosopher in Alexandria by the name of John Philoponus (c. 490–570), who, like Al-Ghazali, argued against the Aristotelian idea of an eternal universe.[15] Craig has formulated the *kalam* cosmological argument in three memorable steps:

1. Whatever begins to exist has a cause.
2. The universe began to exist.
3. Therefore, the universe has a cause.

The first step is self-evident; something that *begins to exist* must have a reason for its beginning. We never see things coming into existence for no reason whatsoever. The second step of the argument, as we have just seen, can be defended both scientifically and philosophically. The third step is the logical conclusion of the argument, which follows necessarily from steps one and two. To be successful in refuting the *kalam* argument, an objector must give good reasons why either step one or step two is more likely to be false than true. Otherwise, the argument stands.

We then come to this question: What options do we have for the cause of the universe? It cannot be material (composed of matter or energy) or temporal; otherwise, it would be part of the universe we're trying to account for in the first place. We need something that is itself uncaused, transcends space-time, and has powers of causation. The only entity that can meet these requirements is an immaterial, personal Mind, exactly how monotheists characterize God.

Is this proof of God's existence? The idea of "proof" in the strict sense of the word, that the opposite conclusion is impossible, is something that is extraordinarily rare, whether we're talking about science, God, or most anything else other than mathematics. What we can say with great confidence is that the evidence available to us, paired with sound reasoning, makes the existence of God vastly more probable than not. Nevertheless, we don't have to bet the farm on this one argument (relax, chickens). The case for a rational Creator is a cumulative one that has often been compared to the body of evidence collected by a crime-scene investigator.[16] Remember the peg-puzzle analogy from chapter 1? Our finite universe represents one significant piece of the Maker Thesis picture.

We will now turn to another kind of cosmic-level evidence for the mind of the Maker: the fine-tuning of the universe for intelligent life.

A Universe Fine-Tuned for Life and Scientific Discovery

After decades of unfailing dedication and hard work, Mr. Jackson has just made partner at his firm. His promotion includes a substantial raise and, quite unexpectedly, a hefty bonus check for a rather irregular sum: $71,369.21. The senior partners inform him that the amount of a new partner's bonus is calculated based upon years of employment, profitability of the employee's accounts, and other quantifiable considerations. Mr. Jackson is ecstatic; he calls his wife with the news, and to his surprise and delight, she says, "Honey, you take that bonus check and go get yourself that sports car you've been dreaming of for so long."

Right after work that very day, Mr. Jackson deposits his bonus check into his bank account, then stops by a luxury car dealership. He is greeted at the door and offered his favored coffee drink—a triple-shot almond milk cappuccino with a splash of vanilla—which is already made. On the small showroom floor sits one car, the exact model he has admired for months on end. It also happens to be in his favorite colors: metallic candy apple red with saddle brown leather interior.

The salesperson opens the driver's door and invites Mr. Jackson to have a seat inside this jaw-dropping driving machine. At the push of a button, the car comes to life. The climate control is preset to the precise temperature Mr. Jackson likes to keep both his home and office. A music playlist appears on the in-dash screen, and as he scrolls through it, he notices that it includes his top ten all-time favorite songs. The driver's seat needs no adjustment, even though Mr. Jackson is quite a bit below average height. To the left of the steering column is an optional cup holder designed for left-handed drivers, which he just happens to be. When he activates the navigation feature, a map appears, outlining directions to his home from the dealership, even though he hasn't entered his street address. Thrilled with the car, he asks the salesperson for the bottom-line price, with taxes and fees included, and the grand total comes to $71,369.21.

What would be a reasonable reaction in such a situation? "Gee, what lucky coincidences"? Of course not. Mr. Jackson would have to be pretty dense to not realize that the salesperson knew he was coming and was privy to some key information that was used to make the car especially well-suited for the prospective buyer.

When it comes to the parameters of our universe, which make the existence of life possible, we face a much more extreme set of "just right" circumstances than Mr. Jackson did with his new sports car. The more our scientific knowledge grows, the more customized for intelligent life our universe seems to be. The phrase "fine-tuned" refers to the fact that the constants and quantities built into the cosmos must fall within an extraordinarily narrow range for the universe to be life-permitting, and an even narrower one for highly complex rational agents such as human beings. *Constants* are the numbers that, when plugged into the mathematical laws of nature, determine the physical character of the universe. *Quantities* are values that are dictated by the initial conditions of the universe; they are factors upon which the laws of nature operate.[17] These constants and quantities are not products of the laws of nature themselves. Rather, they have been discovered by scientific measurements. A universe in which one or more of these constants or quantities had even a slightly different value would look radically different from ours, and it would almost certainly be sterile.

Fine-tuning in itself is not a controversial point. The majority of cosmologists, regardless of their worldview, openly acknowledge it. In *The Grand Design*, Stephen Hawking remarked, "The laws of nature form a system that is extremely fine-tuned," and "[o]ur universe and its laws appear to have a design that both is tailor-made to support us, and if we are to exist, leaves little room for alteration."[18] Freeman Dyson, a theoretical physicist and mathematician, has said, "The more I examine the universe and the details of its architecture, the more evidence I find that the universe in some sense must have known we were coming."[19] Sir Fred Hoyle even admitted that the fine-tuning exhibited by nature "suggests that a superintellect has monkeyed with the physics."[20]

Let's consider a few examples of cosmic fine-tuning. The force of gravity (which is actually the weakest of nature's forces) is a good one to start with because it affects so many aspects of physical reality. For this discussion, I'll use Isaac Newton's equation for the law of gravitational force, $F=G(m_1 m_2/r^2)$, where (F) is the gravitational force we're trying to find, (m_1) is the mass of one object, (m_2) is the mass of the other object, and (r) is the distance between the two. To illustrate, think of an apple that has just come loose from a tree branch. If we know the mass of the apple (m_1), the mass of planet Earth (m_2), and the distance separating the two, we can calculate the force of gravity between them (F) because the gravitational constant (G) is always the same. For you math geeks out there who are dying to know, the value of (G) is 6.67×10^{-11} m^3 kg^{-1} s^{-2}. For those of you who are allergic to math, don't worry. The point you need to understand is that (G) is a constant, an unchanging number in the equation used to calculate gravitational force.

In what ways would the universe be different if (G) had a slightly different value? Robin Collins, a contemporary expert on fine-tuning, says that if (G) were smaller or larger by an unimaginably tiny fraction—only one part in 10^{60}, "the universe would have either exploded too quickly for stars to form, or collapsed back on itself too quickly for life to evolve."[21] If you cannot fathom a number like 10^{60}, a point of comparison would be the estimated number of subatomic particles in the entire known universe: roughly 10^{80}. (The known universe has a diameter of about 92 billion light-years [1 light-year = 5.9 trillion miles].) The point is that if (G) had been off by only an infinitesimal amount, the consequences would be disastrous. Moreover, (G) needs to be extremely weak compared to the other forces of nature; otherwise, there would have been no long-living stars or stars hot enough to provide the necessary energy to support the naturalistic evolution and sustenance of rational life-forms (whether or not the theory of naturalistic evolution is true is totally beside the point here).

There are quite a few other examples of fine-tuning, some of them much more extreme than the case of the gravitational constant. A 1998 observation showed that not only is the universe expanding, its expansion is speeding up. It turns out that there is a mysterious force driving this acceleration; current evidence points to something called *dark energy* as the best candidate. The basic idea is that this dark energy pervades the universe, giving rise to the antigravity repulsion that's causing the expansion of the universe to accelerate. Though cosmologists aren't exactly sure what it is (hence its intriguing name), it makes up about

73 percent of the energy in the universe and is fine-tuned to an extraordinary degree.[22]

The physics involved in investigating the identity of dark energy is complicated to say the least, but here it will suffice to say that in a universe whose dark energy strength was higher by a magnitude of only one part in 10^{120}, space would expand so quickly that there would be no planets or stars. Instead, there would be a very thin mixture of hydrogen and helium atoms. We wouldn't be here, nor would any other kind of life. If the universe's expansion had been slower due to weaker dark energy, it would have collapsed back onto itself too soon to be life-permitting. As Luke Barnes and Geraint Lewis, astrophysicists at the Sydney Institute for Astronomy, have put it, "With dark energy, a universe is rather easy to ruin."[23]

> When all these extreme improbabilities are multiplied together, the idea that the universe is the way it is by sheer chance seems preposterous.

Here are a few more examples of finely tuned features of the universe. You may recall from your high school chemistry class that atoms, the building blocks of matter, are made up of a nucleus containing protons and neutrons and a cloud of orbiting electrons. The strong nuclear force constant, which governs the degree of stickiness between the protons and neutrons in the nucleus, would prevent the existence of life if it were only about 5 percent stronger or weaker. If the electromagnetic force constant, which dictates how strongly atomic nuclei hold on to their electrons, were just a tiny bit different, there would be no life. The mass of neutrons is another crucial value. As astrophysicist Hugh Ross has pointed out:

> If the neutrons were just another 0.1% more massive, so few neutrons would remain from the cooling off of the big bang that there would not be enough of them to make the nuclei of all the heavy elements essential for life...If the

neutrons were 0.1% less massive, so many protons would
be built up to make neutrons that all the stars in the universe would have rapidly collapsed into either neutron
stars or black holes. Thus for life to be possible in the universe, the neutron mass must be fine-tuned to better than
0.1%.[24]

There are dozens of other cosmic parameters that are fine-tuned for
life, and the more cosmologists learn about the universe, the longer
the list grows.[25] When all these extreme improbabilities are multiplied
together, the idea that the universe is the way it is by sheer chance seems
preposterous.

You may be wondering: Perhaps a universe with different constants
and quantities would prohibit life as we know it, but what about types
of life that we cannot even imagine? Barnes and Lewis warn against
playing the "science fiction card" to avoid the implications of fine-
tuning: "Any genesis of life we consider must be based in science, not
science fiction. Any universe in which life can arise must provide the
conditions for the storage and processing of information; a thin soup
of only hydrogen and helium simply does not provide this."[26]

So why is it that the universe exhibits such remarkable fine-tuning?

The Multiverse Solution

Some materialists have attempted to eliminate the fine-tuning
problem by suggesting that our universe is just one of a vast ensemble
of worlds—a so-called multiverse. The idea is that, by some unknown
mechanism operating from eternity past, countless universes are continually generated, each with a random set of physical constraints. Our
universe is simply one of the very few cosmic lottery winners in which
the constants and quantities of nature happen to be those necessary for
the existence of complex life. Proponents of the multiverse argue that,
given an infinite number of successive chances, sooner or later your
ticket will be a winner.

In the previous section, we saw why the concept of a multiverse suffers from an inescapable problem: the impossibility of an infinite series of events. If universes are being generated in any sort of succession, this cannot have been going on forever in the past, because the birth event of our universe would never be reached. Another major weakness of multiverse theory is that there's simply no empirical evidence for the right kind of multiverse (infinite with randomly ordered constants and quantities). But the fact that a model can be built doesn't mean it reflects physical reality. It should be understood that the proposal of the multiverse hypothesis is, by and large, a philosophical move. George Ellis, a physicist and emeritus professor at University of Cape Town, says,

> The universe might be pure happenstance—it just turned out that way. Or things might in some sense be meant to be the way they are—purpose or intent somehow underlies existence. Science cannot determine which is the case, because these are metaphysical issues...Parallel universes may or may not exist; the case is unproved. We are going to have to live with that uncertainty. Nothing is wrong with scientifically based philosophical speculation, which is what multiverse proposals are. But we should name it for what it is.[27]

In a 2016 interview, Ellis said this about the multiverse hypothesis: "It's a problem when scientists present a philosophical statement and claim it can be tested or proved scientifically."[28] But even supposing that a multiverse exists, he says, assuming that they have different laws of nature with different constants and quantities that vary randomly is a baseless assumption.

Did the Universe *Have* to Be This Way?

There is a common perception that if physicists one day achieve a "theory of everything" (TOE), a master theory that would integrate all the fundamental forces of nature into one coherent mathematical system, this would eliminate the problem of fine-tuning by showing that all the constants and quantities of nature *had* to be what they are. This perception is rooted in a misunderstanding. If a TOE is one day completed, it would explain the mathematical interrelationships in physical reality but would not answer the question of why the universe is the way it is, why we have a physically realized TOE that permits the existence of intelligent life. Once again, we see how science necessarily stops short of being able to answer this kind of fundamental philosophical question. Moreover, a successful TOE would further emphasize the deep mathematical rationality of the cosmos—a fact that is, as we shall see, problematic for materialism.

So it seems that the scientist committed to materialism must either say there is simply no explanation for the observed fine-tuning of the universe, that it just is the way it is, or else resort to a theory with no empirical support in an attempt to avoid the conspicuous philosophical implication of fine-tuning: that the universe shows evidence of a designing Mind, a fine-tuner who intentionally ordered it with unfathomable precision.

Key Points

- There is overwhelming scientific evidence for a finite universe, which coincides with philosophical reasons to believe in a cosmic beginning.

- Using these scientific and philosophical reasons as support, a sound argument can be made for the existence of a cause of our universe's beginning—an immaterial, personal agent who transcends space-time.

- The more cosmologists learn about the nature of the universe, the more fine-tuned for life it turns out to be.

- A successful "theory of everything" would not eliminate the fine-tuning problem.
- Cosmic fine-tuning is best explained by the intent of a transcendent Mind; alternative explanations, such as the multiverse, are entirely speculative.

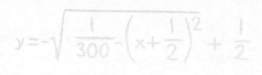

$$y = -\sqrt{\frac{1}{300} - \left(x + \frac{1}{2}\right)^2} + \frac{1}{2}$$

Chapter 4

Priests in God's Cosmic Temple: Natural Revelation and the Scientific Revolution

What if the sun
Be center to the world, and other stars,
By his attractive virtue and their own
Incited, dance about him various rounds?[1]

John Milton

The wisdom of God is exceedingly vast and cannot
be confined to the genius of any one human...For
what we know is only a glimmer. Therefore, wisdom is
to be read in the immense book of God, which is the
world, and there is always more to be discovered.[2]

Tommaso Campanella

I t has been my experience that materialist proponents of the natural sciences become rather irritated when someone brings up the fact that most of the great fathers of modern science were Christian theists. Typically I will raise this point whenever someone claims that a theistic worldview is irrational or that the idea of a Maker of all things is antiscience. The response I receive is almost always something along the lines of "Yes, those were brilliant men of science, but there was so much they did not know—that we now know—about the natural world. They were products of their time. If they lived today, it's likely that none of them would be religious. It's pointless to bring them up in defense of the compatibility of science and faith."

There are several problems with this response, but the one that I find most glaring is the unfounded presumption that men such as Copernicus, Galileo, Kepler, Newton, and Boyle believed in a creator God based upon a lack of scientific knowledge. This misconception betrays an ignorance about the actual writings of these great thinkers, writings which clearly show that it was their discoveries—an increase in knowledge—that incited their written expressions of praise and reverence for an ingenious, omnipotent Maker in whose image mankind is made. Thanks to several major discoveries, it increasingly appeared that the cosmos was crafted in a manner that allowed it to operate according to a pre-ordained set of mathematical laws. The pursuit of knowledge about the workings of the material world was seen as deciphering God's natural revelation, given in his "book of nature." The huge leaps made in natural philosophy during the scientific revolution served to heighten wonder and scholarly appreciation for the rationality of creation and mankind's exclusive ability to understand it.

And So It Began

Essentially, the scientific revolution was launched from the deathbed of Nicolaus Copernicus (1473–1543), a Polish astronomer, mathematician, and church canon who had finally, near the very end of his life, agreed to permit the publication of his major work of natural philosophy, *The Revolutions of the Heavenly Spheres.* His treatise described a mathematical model for a sun-centered (heliocentric) rather than Earth-centered (geocentric) cosmology, which was the long-reigning paradigm. At the time, heliocentrism was not unheard of; back in the third century BC, a natural philosopher known as Aristarchus of Samos had proposed such an arrangement, but the idea had not caught on. Natural philosophers had continued to embrace the geocentric model taught by Aristotle, in which the sun, moon, stars, and planets, embedded in nested transparent spheres, revolved around the earth in perfectly circular orbits.

In the second century AD, the Aristotelian scheme was revised by an Alexandrian natural philosopher by the name of Claudius Ptolemy (c. 100–170), who developed a painfully complicated mathematical model to explain observations of planetary motion in a way that harmonized with geocentrism. By the sixteenth century, the Ptolemaic model had become even messier as astronomers kept adjusting it to better accommodate documented observations of the heavenly bodies.

Copernicus was convinced of heliocentrism not because it enjoyed any more empirical support than the geocentric system, but because it involved a much less cumbersome mathematical model. Retaining the Aristotelian assumption of perfectly circular planetary orbits, he worked out a simpler geometry to explain astronomical observations, but it was no more accurate in terms of predicting future positions of the planets. Copernicus's belief in heliocentrism rested upon philosophical underpinnings; he believed that nature operates with harmonious mathematical regularity and that simpler mathematical descriptions of natural phenomena are more likely to be correct.[3]

In his dedicatory letter to Pope Paul III in the *Revolutions*, Copernicus wrote that the system of the universe is framed for the sake of mankind by "the best and most orderly Artist," who has so precisely arranged the spheres of the heavens that "not one of its parts could be removed without throwing the other parts and the whole universe into confusion."[4] Thus Copernicus believed that more elegant mathematical descriptions were closer to the truth about the system designed by the supreme Mind, who desires that mankind come to understand creation.

The Storm After the Calm

Perhaps because of its lack of empirical support, Copernicanism didn't make much of a splash for quite some time. It was more than a half century after the publication of *Revolutions* that Johannes Kepler (1571–1630), a German mathematician and astronomer, formulated a new mathematical theory of heliocentric planetary motion that harmonized exceedingly well with the (anti-Copernican) astronomer Tycho Brahe's extensive compilation of stargazing records. Kepler, who was Brahe's protégé, found that by representing the planetary orbits as ellipses rather than perfect circles, the observational data could be mathematically represented even more simply than Copernicus's and with greatly improved predictive accuracy.

Kepler's laws of planetary motion (published in his 1609 *New Astronomy* and his 1618 *Harmonies of the World*) transformed the field of astronomy into a sophisticated theoretical science. He was convinced that the universe operated according to laws put in place by its Maker, much like a clock is subject to a clockmaker. This went against an ancient Greek idea about nature having some kind of active "soul" in it, producing its motions: "My aim is to say that the machinery of the heavens is not like a divine animal but like a clock (and anyone who believes a clock has a soul give the work the honour due to its maker) and that in it almost all the variety of motions is from one very simple magnetic force acting on bodies, as in the clock all motions are from a very simple weight."[5] Yet the idea of a clockwork universe that ran according to laws of nature in no way weakened Kepler's theistic convictions.

Both a brilliant natural philosopher and a devout Christian of the Lutheran tradition, Kepler was thoroughly convinced that God had intentionally ordered the universe in a way that could be comprehended by the human intellect. This belief is particularly evident in his private correspondence with fellow scholars and other associates. In a letter to the Baron von Herberstein dated May 15, 1596, Kepler declared that "God, like a human architect, approached the founding of the world according to order and rule and measured everything in such a manner, that one might think not art took nature for an example but God Himself, in the course of His creation took the art of man as an example."[6] There are two notable things about this statement: First, that Kepler expressed a conviction that God created the cosmos according to a rational, mathematical plan; and second, that the mind of God and the mind of man must be somehow analogous. He stated this idea more plainly in what are perhaps his most famous words: "To God there are, in the whole material world, material laws, figures and relations of special excellency and of the most appropriate order...Those laws are within the grasp of the human mind; God wanted us to recognize them by creating us after his own image so that we could share in his own thoughts."[7] Later in the same passage, he chastised those who would say it is presumptuous to imagine that God's mind is anything like man's: "Only fools fear that we make man godlike in doing so; for the divine counsels are impenetrable, but not his material creation."[8]

We see that Kepler's idea of natural revelation is centered upon the fact that the natural world is governed by rational laws that are intelligible to mankind, who by investigating nature can think God's thoughts after him. Kepler made these kinds of statements often. In a letter to his former astronomy professor, Michael Maestlin, he wrote, "God, who founded everything in the world according to the norm of quantity, also has endowed man with a mind which can comprehend these norms. For as the eye for color, the ear for musical sounds, so is the mind of man created for the perception...of quantities."[9] He connects this idea with the Christian doctrine of man in a passage from his work *Conversations with Galileo's Sidereal Messenger*, where he says that geometry "shines in the mind of God" and that a "share of it [mathematical understanding] which has been granted to man is one of the reasons why he is in the image of God."[10]

Kepler's unapologetically Christian philosophy of nature—that it is rationally ordered in a manner compatible with the mind of man, a creature made in God's image—harmonized exceptionally well with both early Christian teaching on natural revelation and Pythagorean-Platonic thought about the intelligible structure of the cosmos. Kepler specifically mentioned both philosophers in his writings. In a 1597 letter to Galileo, he remarked that Galileo, in his work in astronomy, is "following the lead of Plato and Pythagoras, our true masters."[11] In *Harmonies of the World*, he maintained that God is the ultimate source of mathematics and quoted Plato, who said that the Creator "practices eternal geometry."[12] Kepler explained that geometry "provided God with the patterns for the creation of the world, and has been transferred to humanity with the image of God."[13]

Kepler considered his life's work—unlocking the mysteries of planetary motion—as an act of worship. He said, "I had the intention of becoming a theologian...but now see how God is, by my endeavors, also glorified in astronomy."[14] By investigating God's natural revelation, the natural philosopher, who is made in God's image, illuminates some of the divine wisdom made manifest in the creation. Kepler said, "The chief aim of all investigations of the external world should be to discover the rational order which has been imposed on it by God, and which he revealed to us in the language of mathematics."[15] He called the universe "our bright Temple of God" and described astronomers as "priests of the highest God in regard to the book of nature."[16]

An associate of Kepler, Galileo Galilei (1564–1642), is a figure who looms large in the history of science and in discussions about the historical interaction between science and Christianity. Like Kepler, Galileo saw his discoveries as further illumination of the book of nature, but, as we will see later on, this wasn't enough to keep him out of trouble with ecclesiastical authorities.

It would be difficult to overstate the value of Galileo's contribution to the scientific revolution. In 1609, he began building a series of telescopes, each one improving upon the previous in its level of magnification. While he was not the original inventor of the device, his ingenuity resulted in a more sophisticated and powerful instrument than the simple spyglass that had inspired him. The celestial phenomena he was able to observe and measure with his telescope, such as the phases of Venus, added empirical support (though not definitive proof) to the heliocentric model. As a result, Galileo became an aggressive proponent of the Copernican system.

Much to the dismay of both academics and Catholic Church leaders, Galileo (himself a devout Catholic) was not content to treat heliocentrism as mere theory—a mathematical model with which his observations aligned; he insisted that it actually described the physical reality of the heavens. The problem with this was that both the Church and the academy of the day were dominated by Aristotelian philosophy, including the geocentric model of the universe. The Church interpreted passages of Scripture (such as Ecclesiastes 1:5) that speak of the sun rising and going down in a literalistic sense, an understanding that was consistent with Aristotelian-Ptolemaic cosmology. Galileo was quite bold in asserting that such passages should be interpreted differently, even though the correct understanding of Scripture was considered, without exception, the Catholic Church's domain.

Galileo unflinchingly argued for the truth of heliocentrism, but by no means saw it as being incompatible with God's special revelation found in the Bible. In a 1615 letter to the grand duchess Christina of Tuscany, he claimed that the academic philosophers were so opposed to him that they were trying to influence church authorities to denounce him as well, by peppering their arguments against him "with quotations from the Holy Scripture, taken from passages which they do not properly understand."[17] He insisted that the Holy Spirit, through Scripture, taught man how to attain salvation, not how to understand astronomy, quoting a Vatican cardinal, who said that "the intention of the Holy Spirit is to teach us how one goes to heaven, not how heaven goes."[18] In other words, Scripture is not a textbook of natural philosophy.

Galileo's undiplomatic refusal to present his work on heliocentrism as a hypothesis, as the Church had requested, and his vitriolic attitude toward the Pope—including publicly humiliating him in print by portraying him as a simpleton—landed him in hot water with the Inquisition. The official charge was suspected heresy. Upon conviction, Galileo was forced to recant his theory and spend his final few years under house arrest, during which he wrote his final book (a work of physics) while living in rather luxurious accommodations.

This unfortunate episode might have turned out quite differently for Galileo had he used much more finesse in his dealings with Church authorities, particularly at a time when Reformation and counter-Reformation tensions were still running high and the Pope was being pressured by Spain to take stronger measures against heretics. To be sure, what happened to Galileo was terribly unjust, but it would be a mistake to see the Galileo affair as a historical clash with science on one side and Christian theology on the other; it was a complex incident that actually had less to do with theology and a whole lot more to do with the people involved and the political climate. Unfortunately, historical myth abounds, and the case of Galileo is often mischaracterized (including erroneous accounts of Galileo being tortured, imprisoned, and even executed) and used to promote the idea that there is, and has always been, warfare between science and Christianity.

Getting back to the science itself, it is important to note that Galileo did not accept elliptical orbits, even though he was well aware of Kepler's model, so his work did not represent the best astronomy of the time. Perhaps this can be marked up to his intransigent attitude about his own research. Moreover, he did not prove heliocentrism conclusively; yet the fact remains that his integrative approach to astronomy, involving both telescopic observations and a mathematical framework for gaining knowledge about the world, was enormously significant for subsequent scientific investigation.

There is little doubt that Galileo viewed his natural philosophy as being supportive of his Christian faith. In a 1623 volume entitled *The Assayer,* he spoke of the natural revelation of a rational Creator in much the same way Kepler did. He saw nature as a book accessible to mankind through the work of natural philosophy: "Philosophy is written in this all-encompassing book that is constantly open before our eyes, that is the universe; but it cannot be understood unless one first learns to understand the language and knows the characters in which it is written. It is written in mathematical language."[19] Thus, the creation is open to the observation and analysis of those who first learn mathematics, the key for unlocking the secrets of nature. In his letter to the grand duchess Christina, Galileo alluded to the two books of divine revelation: "God reveals Himself to us no less excellently in the effects of nature than in the sacred words of Scripture."[20]

Galileo specifically expressed his regard for Pythagorean-Platonic philosophy in *Dialogue Concerning the Two Chief World Systems*, where Salviati (the Copernican character who serves as Galileo's mouthpiece) says, "That the Pythagoreans held the science of numbers in high esteem, and that Plato himself admired human understanding and believed that it partook of divinity, simply because it understood the nature of numbers, I know very well, nor am I far from being of the same opinion."[21] It is clear that Galileo agreed with these ancients who believed that man's aptitude for mathematical reasoning suggested a relationship to the divine source of the mathematically ordered universe.

The English mathematician and astronomer Sir Isaac Newton (1643–1727), often referred to as the founder of modern science, was the genius who stood on the shoulders of his predecessors and achieved unprecedented heights in natural philosophy. His work further emphasized the mathematical rationality of the material world and how remarkable it is that the mind of man is fit to comprehend it. Although some of his theology was not orthodox by Christian standards, the fact remains that his deepest convictions about the material world and humanity's place in it are right in line with the Maker Thesis.

Sir Isaac Newton's work emphasized the mathematical rationality of the material world and how remarkable it is that the mind of man is fit to comprehend it.

In his magnum opus, *Mathematical Principles of Natural Philosophy* (*Principia* for short), a work still hailed as one of the most important scientific treatises of all time, Newton presented his theory of universal gravitation. The idea behind his theory was that the laws governing terrestrial objects are the same laws involved with the mechanics of the planetary orbits. He developed three laws of motion and then applied them to Kepler's laws of planetary movement. The genius of Newton's work was that it established what is now a central tenet of science: that a set of universal principles can be used to explain a broad range of observations. Newtonian physics demonstrated that the same laws at work with an apple falling from a tree and the trajectory of a launched cannonball could be applied to the revolutions of the planets around the sun and the moon around the earth. It was beginning to look very much as if the universe functioned like a grand machine designed to operate according to fixed parameters, rather than needing constant divine intervention for its motions.

Sir Isaac Newton Playing on the Seashore

Sir Isaac Newton showed tremendous humility about his groundbreaking scientific discoveries, comparing the significance of his work to child's play. He once remarked, "I do not know what I may appear to the world, but to myself I seem to have been only like a boy playing on the sea-shore, and diverting myself in now and then finding a smoother pebble or a prettier shell than ordinary, whilst the great ocean of truth lay all undiscovered before me."[22]

Newton believed that one of the important goals of natural philosophy was to formulate convincing arguments for the existence of God.[23] He articulated his conviction that God is reflected in nature in the introduction (known as the "General Scholium") to the *Principia*, where he wrote, "This most beautiful System of the Sun, Planets, and Comets, could only proceed from the counsel and dominion of an intelligent and powerful being."[24] For Newton, this being was none other than the God of Christianity.

Like Kepler and Galileo before him, Newton appreciated the

theistic implications of the fundamentally mathematical structure of nature and its connection with the mind of man. In some of his unpublished scientific papers, it is evident that he regarded the human intellect as resembling God's—though to a very limited degree. He said that "the analogy between the Divine faculties and our own is greater than has formerly been perceived by Philosophers. That we were created in God's image holy writ testifies."[25] Newton considered his own work an investigation into how much of the divine mind could be discovered through the practice of natural philosophy.[26] He realized that natural revelation, in order to function as revelation, requires creatures equipped to comprehend it. For him, human beings detect the divine rationality revealed in nature because they are made in the image of God. Another facet of Newton's argument for this kinship seems to be based upon the fact that God created the world by an act of divine will and the fact that man is endowed with faculties (of similar kind but lesser degree) that enable him to act and create by a movement of personal free will—though man cannot produce anything out of nothing the way the Almighty did.[27]

From Telescopes to Microscopes

Astronomy and physics were not the only areas of major progress in natural philosophy during the scientific revolution. Great discoveries were also being made in what we now refer to as chemistry and biology, discoveries that were seen as further evidence of a Mind responsible for the design of nature. Eminent English chemist Robert Boyle (1627–1691), is an excellent example of this perspective.

Boyle, who is credited with the modern experimental method, was fascinated with the dynamics of the substances he could manipulate in his laboratory and with the astounding intricacies of life that were being revealed by new, higher-magnification microscopes. The dominant figure in English science until Newton (whose work he influenced) stole the show, Boyle was a meticulous and insightful experimenter who promoted an empirical approach to natural philosophy. He contended that observations of the natural world should take precedence over pre-conceived theories when forming conclusions about nature, and he used his experimental activities to further substantiate the mechanical philosophy—the view that nature operates with regularity, according to set laws. His methods and his ability to think outside the box contributed to his stunning success as an experimenter; he continually had his eye out for newfangled instrumentation that could assist his research, and he would often ingeniously appropriate a device meant for one kind of experiment for use in another.

Boyle was a man of passionate Christian faith, and his desire to further illuminate the mechanical philosophy of nature was partly due to his deep conviction that the regularities and harmony of the material world reflected the omniscience and foresight of the Creator, who had made an orderly world intelligible to mankind. Like Kepler, Boyle saw his work as a theological vocation and described natural philosophers as priests who deciphered truths about the natural world—the temple of God. He wrote that "if the world be a temple, man sure must be the priest, ordained (by being qualified) to celebrate divine service not only in it, but for it."[28] For Boyle, discovering and making known how God's wisdom is communicated by nature was a religious act; he described the rational contemplation of nature as the "philosophical worship of God."[29] He carried out his "priestly orders" with great humility and a heart for the poor, whose condition he sought to improve through his work, especially as it applied to medicine and agriculture.

Boyle believed that nature was a legitimate source of knowledge about the mind of God and worked to plumb its mysterious depths through experimentation, dissection, and microscopy. He was particularly impressed by what he saw as evidence for God in the organic realm. As historian of science and religion John Hedley Brooke put it, "That the machinery necessary for life had been packed into the minutest mite was, for Boyle, more astounding evidence for a deity than the larger machinery of the macrocosm."[30] Boyle used the book metaphor to refer to God's revelation of himself in living things, and believed that interpreting this book was enhanced by expertise in natural philosophy:

> There are diverse things in the Book of the Creatures, in which there appear such manifest Impresses of Wisdom, that even according to the popular notions of men, and the superficiall Theories of vulgar Philosophers; 'tis obvious to conclude, that they [are] the effects of an Intelligent cause: and yet the same things upon a more attentive & skillful inspection, afford to a Philosophical Considerer of them, far greater or more convincing evidences of the power, Wisdom & Beneficence of the Divine Author of things.[31]

By "Philosophical Considerer" he means a natural philosopher, who better understands how strongly nature points to a Creator. In terms of the interaction of natural philosophy and special revelation, Boyle's view was that the former helps us comprehend the latter. If the natural philosopher sees any inconsistency between the two, it is either due to a mistake in natural philosophy or a misinterpretation of the related Scripture. What he charmingly called the "Christian Virtuoso" was a skilled natural philosopher who understood how the study of nature supports belief in, and veneration of, the Maker of all things. This idea is concisely conveyed in the title of one of his last published works: *The Christian Virtuoso: Shewing, That by being addicted to Experimental Philosophy, a Man is rather Assisted, than Indisposed, to be a Good Christian.* In the preface of the book, he expressed adamant disagreement with those who claimed that natural philosophy and theology were incompatible, and he then devoted the remainder of the text to explaining why the virtuoso in natural philosophy can also be a good Christian.

Boyle wrote extensively against atheism and, in doing so, strongly favored design arguments—making the case for the existence and wisdom of God based upon the coherence and intricacies of the universe. He thought that it was utter "stupidity or perverseness" to attribute the skillful contrivances of this grand system to blind chance.[32] One of the ways he reasoned for design was by comparing the marvels of the human muscular system to a fine timepiece:

> We justly esteem it a fine peice of workmanship, when through the crystal case of a watch we observe the various motions of the wheels, Ballance, & other parts, that touch one another without interfering [among themselves] or grateing upon the case. But how much more dos it deserve our applause, that such a multitude of muscles of different sizes & shapes, as are found in the human body, should move briskly & vigorously along one another under the skin, without at all hindering each others motions.[33]

Like the many parts of a watch, which move with smooth, synchronized harmony, the muscles of the human body operate with excellent precision. Elsewhere, Boyle used the illustration of a native finding a watch amidst the detritus of a shipwreck. Even though the native would not understand how the parts of the watch were constructed and assembled in such a fashion and for what purpose, he would still conclude that the object was the product of skill and intelligence. Using a metaphor that came to be associated with the mechanical philosophy of nature, Boyle spoke of the world as a grand clock in which the myriad parts are so expertly crafted that, once they are set in motion by their Maker, they proceed according to his design. He had been inspired by a particular clock he encountered during an extended tour of Europe: the astronomical clock at Strasbourg Cathedral, which featured models of the planets and a mechanism that simulated celestial motions.

The harmonious regularities and mathematical structure of the universe, along with the fact that the human mind is fit to investigate its wonders, were compelling evidence for an ingenious Maker who held mankind in special esteem.

Like the great thinkers previously discussed, Boyle was struck by the fact that nature includes a being like man, who, by his sensory and intellectual faculties, can comprehend the world, thereby perceiving the wisdom and power of the Maker:

> [I]t was very congruous that there should be added to the rest of the creation such a creature as man, who by his Intellect, will, and corporeal organs, should be capable to understand that matchles wisdom, and stupendious Power, to relish that admirable goodnes and to return Thanks, and Praises both for the one, and the others.[34]

It is not insignificant that Boyle mentions the human will; he did not expect that the book of nature, as compelling as he and others found it, would, on its own, change the minds of resolved atheists. "The Will and Affections," he wrote, "have so great an influence upon some men's understandings, that 'tis almost as difficult to make them *believe*, as to make them *Love*, against their Will."[35] Although he admitted that arguments from nature might not persuade the committed atheist, he believed that those sincerely and diligently seeking indications of God's existence would surely be helped along by design arguments.

Copernicus, Kepler, Galileo, Newton, and Boyle were key players in the scientific revolution, and all five of them saw the attributes of the cosmos as indicators of a wise Creator in whose image we are made. The harmonious regularities and mathematical structure of the universe, along with the fact that the human mind is fit to investigate its wonders, were, for them, compelling evidence for an ingenious Maker who held mankind in special esteem.

Key Points

- Kepler, Galileo, Newton, and Boyle were all men of devout faith who saw the new knowledge being gleaned from nature as supportive of the existence of a rational Maker.

- The remarkable congruence between the rationality of nature and the intellect of man was seen as evidence for mankind's special place in the created order.

- The practice of natural philosophy was described as a theological vocation in which its practitioners served as "priests" in God's "temple" of the universe.

- Advocates of the mechanical philosophy of nature which emerged during the scientific revolution likened the natural world to devices such as watches and clocks, which are designed by an intelligent maker to operate with great precision.

- Christian natural philosophers of the scientific revolution saw compatibility and even synergy between their work to elucidate nature and their Christian faith.

Chapter 5

Habitable and Discoverable: A World Just Right for Scientists

We are just an advanced breed of monkeys on a minor planet of a very average star. But we can understand the Universe. That makes us something very special.[1]
Stephen Hawking

In a very real sense the cosmos, our Solar System, and our exceptional planet are themselves a laboratory, and Earth is the best bench in the lab.[2]
Guillermo Gonzalez and Jay Richards

The fact that life is balanced on a razor's edge, that our universe is fine-tuned for our existence, is incredible in its own right, but it's not the end of the story—not by far. A diversity of features of the universe, our solar system, the moon, and planet Earth constitute an amazingly beneficial set of conditions that make both intelligent life *and* scientific discovery possible. It turns out that the set of circumstances needed for a scientifically advanced civilization such as ours is actually narrower than those needed for our biological existence.[3] In other words, there are other possible scenarios that would have allowed for intelligent observers (us), but would have been terribly unconducive to the practice of the natural sciences. In those cases, we would have been stuck in a perpetually primitive existence of hunting and gathering, with no clue about the deeper wonders of the world around us.

Yet in a reality that is far stranger than such fiction, we find ourselves in a world where some of the cosmic and planetary conditions that make complex life possible are the very same ones that allow a broad range of sciences to flourish. Consistent with the Maker Thesis, features of the universe and our planetary home appear to be customized for the existence of intelligent creatures *and* scientific activity; it is as if we were *meant* to uncover the secrets of the world around us.

No Fire, No Modern Science

One of my all-time favorite Tom Hanks films is *Cast Away.* No matter how many times I watch it, I still laugh out loud during the scene where Hanks's character finally manages to produce a flame with two pieces of wood and some shreds of dead vegetation. He builds a roaring bonfire on the beach and circles around it in triumphant, tribal-dancing ecstasy: "Fire! Look what I have created! I have made *fire!*" Not only can he now cook his food, he can use the fire as a signal to any boats or aircraft that happen to pass by the remote island on which he's stranded. In his crude circumstances, fire changes things for the better.

In real life, the harnessing of fire shaped the very course of human history, sending it on its scientific trajectory. Charles Darwin called the mastery of fire the greatest advancement, except language, man has ever made.[4] Without it, mankind would not have progressed much beyond wood and stone tools, since fire is essential in metallurgy (the smelting and forging of metals), a technology that gave rise to virtually all others. There would not have been metal tools, glass, electricity, internal combustion engines, scientific instrumentation (telescopes, microscopes, spacecraft, etc.), or computers—all of which make today's science possible. Learning to use fire was not simply a matter of human ingenuity, although intelligence, creativity, and physical dexterity were certainly required. Other conditions, both cosmic and terrestrial, were necessary for the existence of fire and its role in the sciences.

Philosopher of science Robin Collins has argued that our fine-tuned universe is also the most science-friendly, compared to the hypothetical alternative universes that can be derived on paper by varying the values of the constants in the mathematical laws of nature. For example, fire is dependent upon the electromagnetic force constant (one of the properties of the universe that must be fine-tuned for life) falling into a narrow range. If this value were just a little larger or smaller (yet still within life-permitting range), either open wood fires would have been impossible, or rampant forest fires would have been a serious problem. Without just the right kind of fire, Collins says, "it is far less likely that intelligent life forms would learn to forge metals, and thus develop a scientific civilization."[5] Where the electromagnetic force constant is concerned, we find ourselves in an extraordinarily narrow range that allows for both intelligent life and a tool that is indispensable to science and technology. It's a rather peculiar coincidence...and the oddity doesn't stop there.

> Earth's atmosphere sustains both the sciences and the scientist.

If our home planet lacked specific features, it might have been hospitable to complex life but not controllable fire, or vice versa. Earth's atmosphere is a perfect example; it could have had the properties needed to support the right kind of combustion but not animal respiration (or the other way around), but it just so happens to have qualities conducive to both. Our atmosphere has just under 21 percent oxygen, and for every 1 percent increase in this level there would be a 70 percent increase in the probability of forest fires.[6] On the other hand, if oxygen levels were lower, large land-dwellers like humans wouldn't flourish. The level is precisely where it needs to be for both controllable fire and respiration in complex life. Note that the chemical process involved in fire is entirely different from the one by which lungs absorb oxygen, so to have an atmosphere that simultaneously facilitates each so well is quite remarkable. Earth's atmosphere sustains both the sciences and the scientist.[7]

In order for a planet to have the kind of atmosphere ours has, it must be rocky and roughly the size of Earth. Biologist Michael Denton explains:

> Its gravity must be strong enough to retain permanently the heavier gaseous elements such as nitrogen, oxygen, and carbon dioxide, but weak enough to permit the initial loss of the lighter volatile elements such as hydrogen and helium. Only on planets of similar mass and size to the Earth's could there exist an atmosphere containing sufficient quantities of oxygen to sustain fire.[8]

Fortunately, we have a planet with the right mass to retain the kind of atmosphere that can support both complex life and fire. "It was this coincidence," says Michael Denton, "that allowed mankind to utilize fire in the first place and set out on his technological journey from the Stone Age to the twenty-first century."[9]

But the proper kind of fire and creatures that can harness it are not enough for the metallurgy science requires; other raw materials must be present. It just so happens that the earth's crust is rich in metal ores such as iron and copper, which can be smelted at fire temperatures attainable on Earth using natural fuel sources that were accessible to primitive peoples. The temperatures needed for metallurgy are not reached by burning twigs, grasses, or other tender vegetation; wood, which can be used to manufacture charcoal, was key. Without these kinds of raw materials, controllable fire (and beings biologically advanced enough to use it) would not have been sufficient to set the wheels of scientific progress into motion.

In sum, the origin and evolution of science have been dependent upon controllable fire, which in turn is reliant upon a rather finely tuned value of the electromagnetic force constant and a planet with a specific kind of atmosphere. Interestingly, these requirements happen to also be necessary for the kind of complex life capable of using fire. The birth of metallurgy required fire and complex life, as well as accessible, plentiful metal ores with the right chemical properties and the existence of large, woody plants that could be used to produce appropriate fuels. Lo and behold, all these pieces fell precisely into place, leading to the scientific and technological world we enjoy today.

Observing the Cosmos

Mankind has long beheld the expansive beauty and mystery of the starry heavens with a profound sense of awe. One testament to this fact is how far back we can trace the practices of astrology and astronomy—all the way back to the earliest cities in ancient Mesopotamia, around 4,000 years ago. For a long time, what we now call astronomy and astrology weren't carefully distinguished from one another; observers who documented the moon, stars, and planets were often the same ones giving mystical interpretations to their positions and movements. Nevertheless, modern science owes a great debt to these ancient predecessors, who developed early mathematical methods for astronomical mapping and predictions.

Astronomy and astrophysics have come quite a long way, as human knowledge and instruments such as telescopes have been invented and steadily improved. This advancement would not have been possible were it not for certain facts about Earth, its moon, and the solar system—facts that are also important for complex life on our planet. Once again, we see a set of fortunate circumstances that permit both scientific discoveries and creatures capable of making them.

Galileo's Telescope

Italian astronomer and mathematician Galileo Galilei was not the original inventor of the telescope, but (as far as historians know) he was the first to point one skyward in an effort to further natural philosophy. After hearing about a simple instrument that had been constructed by a Dutch eyeglasses maker, Galileo set to work developing a version with higher magnification. With this more sophisticated telescope, he was able to observe the craters and mountains on the moon, sunspots, the moons of Jupiter, and the phases of Venus. Some of his observations provided empirical support (though not definitive proof) of heliocentrism (a sun-centered planetary system), which went against the reigning Aristotelian idea of an Earth-centered universe.

Prior to the invention of the telescope, astronomers depended upon naked-eye observations for information about the sun, moon, stars, and planets. In order to study the heavens, these ancient and medieval sky watchers needed a clear atmosphere; when or if telescopes came about, it would have done no good to point them toward a sky with a continually dense cloud cover (like that of Venus). Fortunately, Earth's atmosphere is transparent and astronomy was born, but there's an interesting twist to the story. It just so happens that the chemical composition of our atmosphere, which is necessary for protection from detrimental radiation and for respiration in big-brained mammals, is one that is almost entirely transparent to the visible light spectrum when skies are clear. As Benjamin Wiker and Jonathan Witt have put it in their outstanding book *A Meaningful World*, "[T]he very transparency of the chemical constituents of our atmosphere provide an optimal window to let in visible light and also an optimal window for gazing out on the beauty of the heavenly host. In sum, Earth is the paragon of laboratories for the paragon of animals."[10]

This is not to say that atmospheric clarity is the *best possible* for the practice of astronomy; while a perfectly cloudless atmosphere might allow for more unobstructed observation, a partly cloudy one is the overall best if complex life and the conditions necessary for the astronomical sciences are to coincide. Not only is the partly clouded atmosphere we have vital for Earth's hydrological cycle and climate regulation in general (which helps life to flourish), it plays a role in the reduction of atmospheric dust, thereby enhancing the visibility of stars and planets. Once again, what's good for complex life is also highly favorable for the investigation of nature.

Besides its clarity and suitability for intelligent life, there's another fascinating quality of Earth's atmosphere that makes our home planet both habitable and conducive to science. Our atmosphere does an excellent job of allowing the type of solar radiation useful for life to penetrate while filtering out most of the dangerous (and even lethal) radiation. Aside from radio waves, the wavelengths of the radiation that passes through to Earth's surface fall between 3,100 to 9,500 Ångstroms (a word that means ten-billionths of a meter), a range that encompasses 40 percent of the sun's radiant energy.[11] The visible light spectrum, which measures 4,000 to 7,000 Å, falls right in the middle. This range is exactly what is needed for high-resolution vision to be possible in living organisms because water and other biological substances strongly absorb, rather than transmit, radiant energy that falls outside of the visual spectrum. As Michael Denton explains,

> [I]t is difficult to imagine what biological substance could be utilized for the construction of a lens sufficiently transparent to transmit and focus the radiation. Our ability to discriminate between different wavelengths in the visual spectrum—i.e., to see colors—is also dependent on the perfect correspondence between the energy levels of electromagnetic radiation in the visual region and those required for photochemical detection by biological systems.[12]

It isn't just that the kind of eye lenses higher animals have wouldn't work well with a different range of radiation, it's that there is not a known alternative material on earth that would suffice under those hypothetical circumstances. Arguing that vision has simply evolved with respect to the kind of radiation available to earthbound creatures misses the key point being made here: The kinds of chemical processes that would be involved in *any feasible type of vision* are dependent upon a specific range of light wavelengths. Fortunately, the kind of sun and atmosphere we have are wonderfully fit for high-resolution, camera-type eyes.[13]

In addition, it turns out that the narrow range of radiation the atmosphere transmits is the one needed to sustain an indispensable link in the food chain: photosynthetic plants. Any possible type of photosynthetic plant needs light conditions very much like those present on Earth. This is due to a fact of basic chemistry: Chemical reactions are typically driven by the same kind of energy because all molecules absorb similar wavelengths of light.[14] These wavelengths fall within the spectrum of visible light; higher wavelength radiation in the X-ray or gamma-ray region of the spectrum destroys molecules, and lower-wavelength radio radiation does not initiate chemical reactions.[15] So the counterclaim that plants could have still evolved by adapting to a different level of radiation (had the atmosphere been different) falls flat; the chemical reactions needed for *any* photosynthetic process wouldn't be feasible.[16] According to Denton, "That the radiation from the sun (and from many main sequence stars) should be concentrated into a minuscule band of the electromagnetic spectrum which provides precisely the radiation required to maintain life on Earth is a very remarkable coincidence."[17]

The point is that all suns and atmospheres aren't created equal, and ours form a combination that is quite optimal for both complex life and advanced vision—two things essential to science. In their book *The Privileged Planet*, Guillermo Gonzalez and Jay Richards refer to this as "one of the most extraordinary coincidences known to science: an eerie harmony among the range of wavelengths of light emitted by the Sun, transmitted by Earth's atmosphere, converted by plants into chemical energy, and detected by the human eye."[18] It is difficult to dismiss this situation as one that can be chalked up to cosmic luck.

Perfect Solar Eclipses

My first memory of a solar eclipse is one that took place May 30,

1984, when I was approaching the tail end of first grade at my suburban North Carolina elementary school. There was a buzz of excitement among the teachers, who had spent the day before explaining the phenomenon to the students. I remember being a bit spooked by the whole thing, as rumor was circulating among my friends that if you looked at an eclipse, even for a second, you would most certainly go blind. At the hour the annular (partial) eclipse was to begin, my teacher closed the blinds on the classroom windows to keep us from looking at it. We all fell silent, and watched as the daylight filtering in around the edges faded for a time and then gradually returned. Though I was fearful, I also had a vague sense of having missed out on something extraordinary. To this day, I've never had the chance to view a solar eclipse other than in pictures or on NASA TV.

Solar eclipses are indeed special, and not simply because of how rarely most people have the chance to experience them in person. Perfect total eclipses, when the moon passes between the earth and the sun and completely shrouds the sun's photosphere (the light-emitting "surface"), have aided scientific discovery in multiple ways, and (are you noticing a trend?) the conditions that make a perfect eclipse possible are also ones that are enormously beneficial to complex life.

One of the more famous examples of an eclipse facilitating scientific discovery is the empirical confirmation of Einstein's theory of general relativity, which proposed that the curvature of space-time around objects—rather than a pulling force *exerted* by objects—is responsible for gravitation. For a rough analogy, imagine rolling a marble across the mat of a level, smooth trampoline; the marble would proceed in a more or less straight line. However, if you were to place a bowling ball in the center of the mat and then try rolling the marble past it, the path of the marble would bend as it encountered the inward curve in the mat caused by the mass of the bowling ball. General relativity predicted that the curved distortion of space around massive bodies such as the sun would slightly bend beams of starlight that pass by in transit to Earth.

The first empirical support for this prediction came from Arthur

Eddington's photographs of a 1919 solar eclipse, and additional confirmation was provided by images of a 1922 eclipse. A comparison of the photos of the stars in a specific region of the night sky with photos of that same region during the solar eclipses, when the visible light from those same stars passed by the sun during the daytime, showed that the gravity of the sun was indeed bending the light beams, causing the positions of the stars to appear abnormally shifted when viewed by Earth-bound observers. To use the earlier analogy, the sun is like the bowling ball, and the beams of starlight are like the path of the rolling marble.

Newton's Rainbow

In a famous 1666 experiment, recorded in his *Opticks*, Sir Isaac Newton demonstrated that visible light is comprised of a spectrum of colors (though he wasn't the first to know about this). Using two triangular prisms, Newton was able to show that the rainbow of colors appearing when sunlight passes through a prism are not the result of impurities in the glass or crystal, but elements of the light itself, separated out through refraction. When the light passed through the first prism, the spectrum of colors appeared, but when the rainbow passed through the second prism, this was reversed. Newton observed that "whenever all those Rays with those their Colours are mix'd again, they reproduce the same white Light as before."[19]

Since Einstein's eclipse-aided triumph, more advanced astrophysical information has been gleaned from various measurements of the chromosphere and corona—the two regions of the sun's outer atmosphere—which are viewable only during a perfect eclipse. For one thing, knowledge about the composition of stars has come from such measurements. You may remember learning about the colors of the visible light spectrum using the acronym Roy G. Biv—red, orange, yellow, green, blue, indigo, and violet. Back in the nineteenth century, scientists developed a tool called a *spectroscope*, which divides light into its various constituent colors (the different wavelengths). When a spectroscope is aimed at a specific source of light, it can reveal what wavelengths are being emitted from that source, and this provides a wealth of information.

Based upon laboratory experiments, it is now known that different atoms and molecules absorb and radiate different wavelengths of light; thus, when they're heated to a certain temperature, they emit different colors. This fact explains how we get fireworks and neon lights of various hues (actual neon gas always glows orange), and why different elements and compounds produce different-colored flames in the chemistry lab. Moreover, colors are an indicator of temperature; "white-hot" is hotter than "red-hot" when it comes to the glow of burning metals, for example. Thanks to these facts, spectrum data from a spectroscope allows scientists to determine the temperature and chemical composition of a distant light source.

Accumulated records of past eclipses also offer the most useful data for determining the rate at which Earth's rotation is slowing down, a deceleration that averages out to 1.78 milliseconds per day over the course of a century. Precise data about the change in the speed of Earth's rotation can be used to determine how the globe has changed in shape over hundreds or thousands of years on account of events such as glacial movement. In addition, it can help historians interpret ancient calendar systems, which allows them to develop a common historical timeline for human history.[20]

Perfect solar eclipses require certain exact physical parameters. First, a planet's moon must be very round (many moons are not) and must orbit at a particular distance from that planet relative to the distance and size of the planet's sun. When these factors are just right, the moon and the sun appear the same size to the terrestrial observer, so that when the moon passes between the planet and its sun, there's a perfect "fit":

The photosphere is blocked out while the usually invisible chromosphere and corona become fully visible. Theoretically speaking, there
could be many different combinations of planet, moon, and sun sizes
that would produce a perfect eclipse so long as the sizes and distances
were in the right mathematical proportions. In our case, the sun is
about 400 times farther away from Earth than the moon is, but because
it is also 400 times larger, it appears to us, from our perspective, that
the sun and moon are equal in size. Out of the dozens of moons that
orbit the other planets in the solar system, ours is the best size, shape,
and orbital distance for a perfect eclipse.[21] The sun appears larger to
Earth-bound observers than to any other planet in our solar system
that has a moon or moons, which means we have a superior vantage
point. In addition, Earth's size and its distance from the sun mean that
our eclipses last long enough for scientific observation, unlike the situation on larger planets farther away from the sun.

Habitability of the planet in question is the other major factor in
the advantageous solar eclipse equation. Yes, Earth enjoys prime conditions for perfect eclipses, but this would be useless without complex life capable of scientific activities! What do the circumstances that
produce useful eclipses have to do with the flourishing of higher life-
forms? For one thing, our supersized moon is large enough to stabilize the tilt of Earth's rotation axis, keeping it between 22.1 and 24.5
degrees (in relation to the plane in which it orbits around the sun)
over the course of millennia. If the moon were only about two percent larger, it would be *de*stabilizing, and the tilt of Earth's axis would
vary widely. Both stability and degree of tilt are important in prevent-
ing drastic climate fluctuations and promoting a global distribution of
rainfall.[22] Not enough tilt, and Earth would have no seasons; too much
tilt, and most of Earth's northern hemisphere would have constant daylight with scorching heat for half the year, and frigid darkness for the
other half. Neither scenario would be life-friendly.

Earth's distance from the sun is also a big deal for life because a planet must orbit its star within certain distance parameters in order to have liquid water. If we were a little closer to the sun, water would dry up; if we were a bit further away, water would be locked up in ice. (Note that atmospheric pressure also contributes to a planet's ability to maintain surface water.) Earth's orbit around the sun falls within what is called the *Circumstellar Habitable Zone* (CHZ), where conditions allow for the presence of liquid water. It has been nicknamed the "Goldilocks Zone"—not too close, not too far away, but just right.

The size of our sun is yet another factor in habitability. If it were much larger, it would exhaust its fuel too quickly; much smaller, and Earth would have to be so close to it that gravitational force would cause one hemisphere of our planet to perpetually face the sun rather than have a twenty-four-hour rotation.[23] This is called *tidal locking*, and would be life-prohibitive, since Earth's surface water would be trapped as ice on the night side of the planet and its protective magnetic field (which deflects harmful radiation) would be weaker.

> Earth's orbit around the sun falls within what is called the *Circumstellar Habitable Zone*...It has been nicknamed the "Goldilocks Zone"—not too close, not too far away, but just right.

Some have argued that Earth's perfect solar eclipses are nothing more than a lucky and passing coincidence. Granted, the moon used to be much closer and is still steadily receding from Earth, which means that perfect solar eclipses from Earth's perspective are only temporary on a cosmic timescale. Moreover, the sun's size and radiation emissions—both crucial to life—change as it ages. However, the temporality of these factors does not diminish how remarkable it is that the flourishing of mankind is occurring during the time when habitability is correlating with discoverability; in fact, it adds another dimension to the problem. Isn't it a curious thing that mankind is thriving during the window of time that perfect eclipses are an available (and invaluable) tool for scientific discovery? "The most habitable place in the Solar System," say Gonzalez and Richards, "yields the best view of solar eclipses just when observers can best appreciate them."[24]

Friendly and Informative Neighbors

Growing up, I longed for a telescope; I was intrigued with stars, comets, and especially the mysterious planets of the solar system. As a child, I had no concept of the wider galaxy, much less the universe as a whole. Yet the sun, moon, and nine planets (yes, we had nine back then, and Pluto will always have a special place in my heart) captured my imagination in a way that little else did. I now find our planetary neighborhood exponentially more interesting in light of what astronomers now know about its role in scientific discovery and how its features have made advanced life on Earth far more probable.

Our remarkable solar system was truly a boon to the scientific revolution. You may recall that Galileo's telescopic observation of the phases of Venus and his discovery of the moons orbiting Jupiter were empirical support for the theory of heliocentrism (a sun-centered cosmos). Kepler was only able to formulate his three laws of planetary motion by using specific data—data obtainable during his time because several planets with a wide range of distances from the sun were observable against a background of fixed stars. Newton was able to build upon the work of Galileo and Kepler, using it as a foundation for his universal laws of motion and theory of gravitation. Then Newton's discoveries gave rise to Einstein's theory of general relativity during the physics boom of the twentieth century, a theory which was tested by a solar eclipse! Our "planetary playpen," as Gonzalez and Richards call it, with its simplicity and regularity, has been absolutely crucial for the progress of physics and astronomy.

Earlier in this chapter, we saw how important the Earth-sun-moon arrangement is for complex life and scientific discovery, but that's only part of the story. The other objects (planets and asteroids) that orbit our sun are also key players, and systems like ours turn out to be quite rare. As astrophysicist Hugh Ross explains:

> Ongoing research has led astronomers to conclude that [for] a planet sufficiently like Earth to be able to sustain advanced life requires a very particular suite of accompanying gas giant planets, a suite that formed in a very particular way. In fact, the more planets astronomers study both inside and outside our solar system and the more models they build in an effort to understand planetary system formation, the more evident the uniqueness of Earth's solar system becomes.[25]

For example, the massive gas giants (Jupiter, Saturn, Uranus, and Neptune), with their powerful gravitational attraction, protect Earth from bombardment by asteroids and comets. If the gas giants were too small or too far away, their protection would be inadequate, and if they were too large or too close, they would interfere with the orbits of the smaller planets of the inner solar system (Mercury, Venus, Earth, and Mars). Moreover, during the formation of our planetary system, the gas giants influenced Earth's size and orbital dynamics, which, as we've already seen, make advanced life possible. The smaller planets of the inner solar system are not inconsequential to Earth, by the way; they (at the least) serve as mechanical shields against asteroids and comets. Had there been too many of them, though, the stability of our system would suffer. "The most habitable and measurable system will be one with the most planets allowed by stability constraints," explain Gonzalez and Richards.[26] This is precisely the kind of system we have.

Even the amount of leftover debris from the formation of the solar system—now collected in the asteroid belt between Mars and Jupiter—helps make Earth life-friendly. The vast majority of other systems lack asteroids, while a much smaller number of them have much larger belts. Asteroids deliver essential elements to Earth on impact, but too many collisions would be catastrophic. Fortunately, Mars, which lies between the asteroid belt and Earth, is not so massive that it steers a higher number of asteroids toward our planet. A bonus is that the size of Mars is good for astronomy: A larger Mars would reflect more sunlight, significantly inhibiting our observations of more distant celestial bodies, just as a brightly moonlit night interferes with our ability to see the stars.[27]

The Copernican Cliché

In *The Revolutions of the Heavenly Spheres*, Nicolaus Copernicus challenged the earth-centered (geocentric) cosmology of Aristotle, which had been the consensus among academics and churchmen alike throughout the Middle Ages. Unfortunately, it is a common and long-running misperception that Copernicanism, once confirmed, dethroned Earth from a privileged place in the cosmic scheme and showed us that mankind is not central in importance. In other words, geocentrism is unaccountably equated with anthropocentrism (human-centeredness). This idea grew into the historical myth that claims Copernicus inadvertently helped drive the first nail into God's coffin. The truth is, Aristotelian natural philosophy prior to Copernicus considered Earth to be the "lowest" point in the universe, a sort of garbage dump where heavier, baser elements settled. Being removed from the center and elevated to move among the uncorrupted celestial bodies—the other planets and stars—was actually, according to the philosophy of the time, a wonderful promotion for Earth.

This is a mere sampling of the many criteria necessary for a universe, solar system, and home planet to be as supportive of both complex life and scientific discovery as ours happen to be. Taking the myriad of factors into account, it seems much more probable than not that intelligent life on Earth and conditions favorable to science were *intended* to coexist, that creatures who could learn something of the rational plan of the cosmos and thereby sense their kinship to their Maker were intended (the Maker Thesis).

Some have responded that we shouldn't be surprised to see that our home enjoys such fortunate physical circumstances, because otherwise we wouldn't be here to observe them. This objection to the habitability-discoverability argument misses the point entirely. Of course we wouldn't be here without life-sustaining conditions, but the real questions are, Why do so many factors harmonize in just the right way, and why does habitability for complex life correspond with such a high level of discoverability? Even if it is one day found that there are other systems much like ours, this doesn't weaken the habitability-discoverability argument. These big *why* questions arise from the scientific data, but transcend science's ability to answer them. Earth may not be at the geometric center of the universe or even the solar system, but atheist Carl Sagan was quite mistaken when he said that Copernicus delivered a "great demotion" to the significance of mankind with the theory of heliocentrism.[28] Our place in the cosmos is, in fact, extraordinarily advantageous.

> Taking the myriad of factors into account, it seems much more probable than not that intelligent life on Earth and conditions favorable to science were *intended* to coexist, that creatures who could learn something of the rational plan of the cosmos and thereby sense their kinship to their Maker were intended.

Key Points

- Not only is the universe finely tuned for life, it has the necessary attributes required for the activities of scientific discovery. The overlap between habitability and discoverability is remarkable.

- Due to its role in metallurgy, fire that could be harnessed by primitive man was essential for the beginning of science as we know it. There is a very narrow range of cosmic and terrestrial conditions that make fire, metallurgy, and complex life possible.

- The kind of atmosphere Earth has is necessary for the respiration of complex life and protection from lethal cosmic radiation; moreover, its chemical composition provides the optical clarity necessary for astronomy.

- Photosynthetic plants (of any possible kind) require light that also happens to fall within the wavelength range visible to humans. The kind of sun and atmosphere we have provide just the right kind of light.

- Perfect solar eclipses, which have been vital to science, are made possible by many of the same conditions that allow for complex life on earth. Humans exist during the temporary window of time in which Earth can have perfect solar eclipses.

- The other bodies in the solar system are a support system for complex life on Earth, and their arrangement has been key in many discoveries, especially from the scientific revolution onward.

Chapter 6

A Death Knell for Design Arguments? Natural Theology and Darwin's Response

> To my mind it accords better with what we know
> of the laws impressed on matter by the Creator,
> that the production and extinction of the past
> and present inhabitants of the world should
> have been due to secondary causes...[1]
>
> *Charles Darwin*

> A law presupposes an agent; for it is only
> the mode, according to which an agent
> proceeds: it implies a power; for it is the order,
> according to which that power acts.[2]
>
> *William Paley*

As discussed in chapter 1, the Maker Thesis does not involve challenging or supporting the theory of common descent—the tenet of Darwinism as well as modern evolutionary theory that says all living things have descended from a common biological ancestor. When it comes to the existence of God and his image in mankind, the question of evolutionary common descent is beside the point. It is merely a theory about biological history and cannot say anything about immaterial realities or about the historicity of those Scripture refers to as Adam and Eve. However, many people today are under the mistaken impression that scientific evidence that is deemed supportive of common descent is automatically corrosive to design arguments and inconsistent with belief in some doctrinal essentials. Thus, before examining biological design arguments and how they contribute to the Maker Thesis, it will be helpful to first understand how design arguments were historically used, Charles Darwin's response, and the subsequent reactions of some scientific Christian theists of his time. We will see that it wasn't the idea of common descent per se that threatened design arguments for the existence of a Maker or man's special place in the world; rather, it was the materialist philosophical framework being unnecessarily imposed upon evolutionary theory—a dynamic that has persisted in the contemporary debate.

The Heyday of Natural Theology

The 1859 publication of Charles Darwin's explication of his theory of evolution, *The Origin of Species*, appeared during natural theology's prime, when scientists, philosophers, and theologians often cited the intricacy of living organisms as evidence for a divine Maker. Nowadays, it is said that the genius of Darwin was his development of a plausible account of design that didn't require a personal designer, and therefore his theory spelled the demise of natural theology. As evolutionary biologist Ernst Mayr (1904–2005) once said, "Explaining the perfection of adaptation by materialistic forces (selection) removed God, so to speak, from his creation. It eliminated the principal arguments of natural theology, and it has been rightly said that natural theology as a viable concept died on November 24, 1859."[3]

In order to determine whether or not statements like Mayr's are accurate, one must first understand design argumentation prior to Darwin's work. During the first several decades of the eighteenth century, the systematic study of nature was thoroughly steeped in natural theology. It was not uncommon for scientific books and papers analyzing the natural world to contain praises to the Creator for his ingenious handiwork. The more prominent natural theologians were extraordinarily well-read in natural philosophy (what we now refer to as the natural sciences), even if that was not their primary area of scholarship.

Reams of books, tracts, and sermons promoting design arguments sprouted within this philosophical and religious climate, but the idea that God and his wisdom are revealed in nature did not go unchallenged. The most renowned of these challenges came from the skeptical philosopher David Hume (1711–1776) in his *Dialogues Concerning Natural Religion*, a work not published until after his death. In the *Dialogues*, Hume uses a conversation between three speakers to deliver his critique of design arguments. For present purposes, it is sufficient to note two of his main objections: (1) that the natural world doesn't bear a sufficient resemblance to human artifacts (like clocks, to use one of Hume's examples) to justify drawing analogies for design arguments; and (2) since we can know nothing about the nature of God's mind, it is impossible to infer divine intelligence from what we perceive as "marks of wisdom" in nature; to do so is anthropomorphism—making God manlike by assuming man's notions about design are analogous to God's.

Whether or not Hume's negative assessment of design arguments truly succeeds (and if so, to what degree) has been a matter of debate ever since the *Dialogues* rolled off the press. The claim that "Hume demolished design once and for all" is now rampant in popular writing (and appears in more sophisticated form in various scholarly sources), but this widespread perception did not come about until much later. Many of Hume's scholarly contemporaries were not persuaded, rejecting his critique on philosophical grounds, and some of today's scholars remain similarly unmoved by Humean arguments against the detection of design in nature. In any case, in the decades following the publication of the *Dialogues*, design arguments continued to be widely used, even by some who were well acquainted with Hume's book.

By far the most influential work that was intended as a counterpoint to Hume was Paley's *Natural Theology.* William Paley (1743–1805) was a brilliant student at Christ's College, Cambridge, where he studied mathematics and won several prestigious scholarships and other academic prizes. He was appointed a fellow and tutor of his college after graduating from his program as "senior wrangler" (the top student in mathematics), a distinction that was, at the time, considered the greatest intellectual achievement in all of England. Early in his ensuing teaching career, Paley was ordained as a deacon in the Church of England and then as a priest following his election as a fellow of his college. He eventually left the halls of academia to pursue a career as an Anglican clergyman yet continued his scholarly activities, which included writing and publishing on subjects such as moral philosophy, apologetics, and history. *Natural Theology* was his final work, published in 1802, just a few short years before his death. Its objective was to show the continuing value of design arguments (contrary to Hume's analysis decades prior) and the compatibility of natural philosophy and orthodox Christianity.

Paley opened his book with the well-known watchmaker discourse. Although the comparison of aspects of nature with a time-keeping device was by no means his original idea, the metaphor went on to become constantly associated with his name: Paley's watchmaker. His presentation of the argument is quite eloquent and deserves to be quoted in full:

> In crossing a heath, suppose I pitched my foot against a stone, and were asked how the stone came to be there, I might possibly answer, that, for any thing I knew to the contrary, it had lain there forever...But suppose I had found a watch upon the ground, and it should be enquired how the watch happened to be in that place, I should hardly think of the answer which I had before given, that, for anything I knew, the watch might have always been there. Yet why should not this answer serve for the watch as well as for the stone? Why is it not as

admissible in the second case, as in the first? For this reason, and for no other, viz. that, when we come to inspect the watch, we perceive (what we could not discover in the stone) that its several parts are framed and put together for a purpose, e.g. that they are so formed and adjusted as to produce motion, and that motion so regulated as to point out the hour of the day; that, if the several parts had been differently shaped from what they are, of a different size from what they are, or placed after any other manner, or in any other order, than that in which they are placed, either no motion at all would have been carried on in the machine, or none which would have answered the use, that is now served by it.[4]

Paley's point was that a watch, unlike a stone, is evidently *made for a purpose*: tracking the passage of time. He went on to describe the springs and gears that produce motion in the watch, allowing it to carry out its intended function, and noted the precision and foresight required to devise such an intricate, functional marvel. He said that "the inference...is inevitable; that the watch must have had a maker; that there must have existed, at some time and at some place or other, an artificer or artificers who formed it for the purpose which we find it actually to answer."[5]

Ancient Roots of the Clock Metaphor

The comparison of the orderly cosmos with a clock dates back at least as far as the first century BC writings of the famous Roman orator Cicero. In his dialogue entitled *The Nature of the Gods*, the character Balbus, who is representative of the Stoic view, argues:

> But if all the parts of the universe have been so appointed that they could neither be better adapted for use nor be made more beautiful in appearance, we must investigate whether

this is accidental, or whether the condition of the world is such that it certainly could not cohere unless it were controlled by the intelligence of divine providence...It can surely not be right to acknowledge as a work of art a statue or a painted picture, or to be convinced from distant observations of a ship's course that its progress is controlled by reason and human skill, or upon examination of the design of a sundial or a water-clock to appreciate that calculation of the time of day is made by skill and not by chance, yet none the less to consider that the universe is devoid of purpose and reason, though it embraces those very skills, and the craftsmen who wield them, and all else besides. [6]

For Balbus, it is absurd to see the universe as the product of blind chance rather than rational skill because the world bears marks of intentional design, as do water clocks and sundials—the time-keeping mechanisms of his day.

Historian of science Dr. James Hannam has argued that the clock metaphor used by natural theologians such as William Paley is connected to early mechanical clocks, which most likely appeared sometime during the thirteenth century. These clocks (which were not very reliable timekeepers) had mechanisms that were used to power armillary spheres—astronomical models that showed the positions of the planets (with the earth, rather than the sun, at the center). Thus it was only one small step in reasoning to draw an analogy between the actual universe and these kinds of devices, which were known to have been designed by a rational agent. [7]

Paley dedicates the majority of his book to an exposition of the elegant complexity of biological structures, which he refers to as "contrivances"—intentional assemblages of parts. Probably best known of them all is his description of the eye, the first example he gives of a biological organ that shows evidence of having been designed for a specific end—namely, sight. He likens the eye to a familiar human artifact:

> As far as the examination of the instrument goes, there is
> precisely the same proof that the eye was made for vision,
> as there is that the telescope was made for assisting it. They
> are made upon the same principles; both being adjusted to
> the laws by which the transmission and refraction of rays
> of light are regulated.[8]

Thereafter, Paley builds a cumulative case for design based upon the physiology of human beings, animals, insects, and plant life. He seeks to reinforce the idea that there are features of living organisms that are analogous to manmade mechanisms.

Natural Theology contains only one short chapter on the subject of physics and astronomy, but it offers interesting insights that make it worth mentioning. Paley doesn't consider the system of planetary and stellar motion ideal for the type of argument he is making because there is no analogous human invention with which to compare it. Nonetheless, he acknowledges that astronomical phenomena can be used to reinforce one's conclusion of a designing Creator, for they show "beyond all other sciences, the magnificence of his operations" and raise the mind "to sublime views of the Deity."[9] He remarks, almost in passing, that the fact that the solar system is law-governed is "sufficient to indicate an intellectual agency."[10] This observation would go on to become central in the much later revival of natural theology.

Paley's cursory treatment of force and gravitation contains nothing novel; thus, it is unsurprising that it is typically ignored in discussions of the watchmaker argument. However, nestled inconspicuously within this very chapter is a statement that deserves careful attention:

> The real subject of admiration is, that we understand so
> much of astronomy as we do. That an animal confined
> to the surface of one of the planets; bearing a less propor-
> tion to it, than the smallest microscopic insect does to the

plant it lives upon; that this little, busy, inquisitive creature, by the use of senses which were given to it for its
domestic necessities, and by means of the assistance of
those senses which it has had the art to procure, should
have been enabled to observe the whole system of worlds
to which its own belongs...all this is wonderful, whether
we refer our admiration to the constancy of the heavenly
motions themselves, or to the perspicacity and precision
with which they have been noticed by mankind.[11]

Paley's argument here centers on the astonishing fact that man, as small
as he is in comparison with the universe, has the sensory and rational capacities—what he calls the powers of "exactest observation" and
"acutest reasoning"—to perform the complex calculations needed to
describe and predict astronomical movement. The implicit claim is
that man must have an honored place in the created order; he possesses
a rationality that far surpasses what is needed for survival and reproduction ("domestic necessities"), one that allows him to mathematically investigate the universe. Near the end of the book, Paley reiterated
the exceptional nature of man: "The degree of understanding found in
mankind, is unusually much greater than what is necessary for preservation," a statement that, as we shall see, remarkably anticipated the
materialist claims of Darwinism and subsequent counterarguments.[12]
Paley's insights serve as yet another contribution to two major themes
of the Maker Thesis: a rational cosmos that is, remarkably, intellectually accessible to the mind of man.

> The features of nature...make the existence of an intelli-
> gent Creator far more likely than any opposing theory that
> says undirected natural processes *alone* are responsible
> for the amazingly complex and purposeful mechanisms
> found in nature.

Paley was well aware of the fact that his arguments did not provide unassailable proof of the existence of God. He rightly saw the case for a Creator as a cumulative, probabilistic argument, just as the best scientific theories of his time and ours are. He was convinced that the features of nature (and of the natural philosophers who work to comprehend them) make the existence of an intelligent Creator far more likely than any opposing theory that says undirected natural processes *alone* are responsible for the amazingly complex and purposeful mechanisms found in nature. By Paley's time, evolutionary scenarios were already much discussed as possible routes that would avoid the need to invoke special creation as an explanation, but a crucial and often overlooked fact is that Paley offered a clear "even if" statement regarding gradualistic accounts of natural history, what he called "secondary causes" at work in the world. He suggested that even if the material world possesses properties that have naturally driven a long chain of events leading up to what can be presently observed, that does absolutely nothing to weaken the case for design:

> If, in tracing these causes, it be said, that we find certain general properties of matter, which have nothing in them that bespeaks intelligence, I answer, that, still, the managing of these properties, the pointing and directing them to the uses which we see made of them, demands intelligence in the highest degree... There may be many second causes, and many courses of second causes, one behind another, between what we observe of nature and the Deity; but there must be intelligence somewhere; there must be more in nature than what we see; and, amongst the things unseen, there must be an intelligent, designing, author.[13]

By "second causes" Paley meant what we would typically refer to as natural mechanisms; he recognized that such causes—even long strings of them—do not lessen the need for a primary cause (the Creator). He explained that being able to describe inherent organizing principles of matter (potentialities) and the resulting natural processes does not do away with the need for an intelligence behind the phenomena. To clarify his meaning, he used the illustration of the manufacturing of cloth by machinery that does the work of spinning and weaving threads into various fabrics. We cannot point to the process by which the textiles are generated and thereby "pretend to dispense with intention, thought, and contrivance, on the part of the artist; or to dispense, indeed, with the necessity of any artist at all, either in the manufactory of the article, or in the fabrication of the machinery by with the manufactory was carried on."[14]

In the same way, any natural physical processes responsible for the production of what Paley calls biological "contrivances" suggests intelligence behind the mechanisms themselves. Adding intermediate steps between the original intelligent agency and the finished product doesn't lessen the necessity of the creative Mind who is ultimately responsible for it all. Concerning those thinkers who attempt to rule out design in nature, he said they are showing a philosophical precommitment in their "endeavour to dispense with the necessity in nature of a particular, personal, intelligence; that is to say, with the exertion of an intending, contriving mind, in the structure and formation of the organized constitutions which the world contains."[15]

The reception of Paley's *Natural Theology* was the stuff of publishers' dreams. It went through many editions over many years; it would be difficult to overestimate its intellectual influence. One of its most renowned readers was captivated by the Palean argument, but later came to be its most formidable detractor.

Darwinism: The Death of Design and the Demotion of Man?

In the College Hall of Christ's College at Cambridge, William Paley has been immortalized in a beautiful stained glass window portrait. The portrait facing Paley's—and paired with it in a manner that makes the two windows seem like two sides of a visual story—depicts a later student of the college: none other than Charles Darwin.

Like Paley, Darwin entered Cambridge with an expectation of

being a clergyman; such a career would afford him the time and the resources to pursue his work as a naturalist—collecting, examining, and writing about biological specimens. In the Victorian era, this bivocational arrangement was not uncommon; shepherding a parish was a respectable way for men of the cloth to support themselves and still have the necessary time and resources to enjoy the intellectual stimulation offered by natural philosophy. In his autobiography, which he began writing just a few years before his death, Darwin recalled that he rather liked the idea of being a "country clergyman," though he had some initial reservations about declaring his agreement with all the dogmas of the Church of England.[16] Even so, after reading several theological works, he became satisfied with "the strict and literal truth of every word in the Bible" and proceeded through a course of study that included mathematics, classics, and William Paley's major works.[17]

Darwin lamented that what he called the "academical" studies (mathematics and classics) were sadly wasted upon him, since even with the help of a (very boring) tutor, he performed poorly in mathematics, mostly because of his attitude and lack of motivation. He said, "This impatience was very foolish, and in after years I have deeply regretted that I did not proceed far enough at least to understand something of the great leading principles of mathematics; for men thus endowed seem to have an extra sense."[18] He also admitted to being negligent in his attendance of the classics lectures that were part of his curriculum (though it should be noted that he did brush up on classical studies and develop a love of Euclidean geometry before finishing his degree). Conversely, Darwin devoured Paley's *Evidences of Christianity*, *Moral Philosophy*, and *Natural Theology* with sharp attention to detail. About the third book he said, "The logic...of his *Natural Theology* gave me as much delight as did Euclid."[19]

That Time Darwin Tasted a Bug

Though he was not the most ambitious student, often

neglecting his studies in favor of his shooting hobby, Darwin's zeal for the study of nature was intense and his desire to unlock its mysteries insatiable. Early on, he loved to collect and name new species of beetles, and in his autobiography he told a hilarious story about one very memorable beetle-hunting escapade:

> [O]ne day, on tearing off some old bark, I saw two rare beetles and seized one in each hand; then I saw a third and new kind, which I could not bear to lose, so that I popped the one which I held in my right hand into my mouth. Alas it ejected some intensely acrid fluid, which burnt my tongue so that I was forced to spit the beetle out, which was lost, as well as the third one.

Talk about devotion to one's science!

Several months after taking his degree at Cambridge, Darwin embarked upon a five-year voyage that would determine the course of the rest of his life and impact the world of science forevermore. He was granted a spot as a naturalist aboard the HMS *Beagle*, which set sail in December of 1831. In the ports he visited (which included the exotic Galapagos Islands), he studied the local flora, fauna, and geology, collecting as many specimens as he could and meticulously documenting his observations. His passion for shooting, which dominated his free time before and during his Cambridge years, came in handy, as this was how he obtained many birds and animals for his growing collection. Once he returned to England, Darwin consulted with various scholarly associates about his specimens and written records from his excursion and worked on organizing and editing his field notebooks. He then spent years pondering and developing the theory that he introduced to the world in his 1859 treatise *On the Origin of Species*—the theory of evolution by natural selection.

As mentioned earlier, many claim that Darwin's great contribution to science was a naturalistic explanation for the complexity and diversity of plant and animal species—an explanation that eliminated the need to postulate special creation. In a nutshell, Darwin argued that variations in living organisms are naturally selected through the struggle and competition for survival. This is where the phrase "survival of the fittest" comes from. The idea is that organisms born with beneficial characteristics (caused by natural principles of variation) survive and reproduce better, and over time, their traits spread throughout their population. Eventually, after many generations over vast stretches of time, natural selection brings about an altogether new species. Supportive of Darwin's theory was the fact that the fossil record seemed to bear testament to a succession of species—plants and animals that lived for a time and then died out as they were replaced by new ones. This indicated that nature is not static, as some natural theologians believed. Instead, it changes over time, with entire species passing out of existence as they are supplanted by new, better-adapted ones.

Darwin envisioned natural history as a great tree with branches that bore multiple limbs representing species gradually diverging from one another, some terminating as side branches and some continuing upward and diversifying even further. In a particularly poetic passage in the *Origin*, he wrote: "As buds give rise by growth to fresh buds, and these, if vigorous, branch out and overtop on all sides many a feebler branch, so by generation I believe it has been with the great Tree of Life, which fills with its dead and broken branches the crust of the earth, and covers the surface with its ever branching and beautiful ramifications."[20] Darwin theorized that all life-forms arose from a common ancestor (the root of the tree), and that "probably all the organic beings which have ever lived on this earth have descended from some one primordial form, into which life was first breathed."[21] It's difficult to miss his allusion to the Genesis account of creation.

By the time his *Origin* was published, Darwin had abandoned orthodox Christian faith, but he retained a universalist flavor of theism. He used quite a lot of creation-friendly language in his case for common descent by natural selection, though there is debate about whether he was sincere in this or was simply pandering to Victorian sensibilities of his time. The page facing the title page of the first edition of *Origin* bore the following "two books" quote from eminent natural philosopher Francis Bacon's *Advancement of Learning*: "To conclude, therefore, let no man out of weak conceit of sobriety, or an ill-applied moderation, think or maintain, that a man can search too far or be too well studied in the book of God's word, or in the book of God's works; divinity or philosophy; but rather let men endeavour an endless progress or proficience in both."

In 1871, Darwin published *Descent of Man*, the work in which he discussed how his theory of common descent by way of natural selection applies to human origins. His overarching point was that mankind is different only in degree, not in kind, from the rest of the animal kingdom. In other words, there is nothing about the constitution of human beings that makes them fundamentally distinct from other creatures; they are merely more highly evolved apelike animals, not the intended crown of creation. Darwin dedicated three chapters to his reasons for believing that man's higher cognitive faculties are nothing more than advanced versions of faculties seen in lower animals (most notably the great apes), and that human mental powers simply resulted from a steady, upward march of unguided evolutionary change. Obviously, these conclusions stand in sharp contrast with the Maker Thesis—that the marks of wisdom in living things are evidence of intentional creation and that man's unique faculties for grasping the inherent orderliness of nature is part of the image of God in him. However, in his autobiography (written over a period of years following his *Descent of Man*), Darwin expressed reservations about the complete removal of divine agency from the origin of human rationality:

> Another source of conviction in the existence of God, connected with the reason and not with the feelings, impresses me as having much more weight...This follows

from the extreme difficulty or rather impossibility of conceiving this immense and wonderful universe, including man with his capacity for looking far backwards and far into futurity, as the result of blind chance or necessity. When thus reflecting I feel compelled to look to a First Cause having an intelligent mind in some degree analogous to that of man; and I deserve to be called a Theist.[22]

It is by no means trivial that Darwin was struck by how exceptional man's mental faculties are and how insensible it seems to suggest that such advanced minds came from mindless evolutionary processes rather than an intelligence with whom mankind has kinship. Darwin went on to say that his confidence in this line of reasoning for God's existence waxed and waned over time, ending up weaker than it was when he first penned *Origin*. But then he voiced doubts about the very trustworthiness of our belief formation if man's mind is merely an evolved material brain operating according to deterministic processes:

> But then arises the doubt—can the mind of man, which has, as I fully believe, been developed from a mind as low as that possessed by the lowest animal, be trusted when it draws such conclusions? May not these be the result of the connection between cause and effect which strikes us as a necessary one, but probably depends merely on inherited experience?[23]

It is striking that Darwin saw the problem for human rationality that is inherent to the materialist worldview. He concludes, "I cannot pretend to throw the least light on such abstruse problems. The mystery of the beginning of all things is insoluble by us; and I for one must be content to remain an Agnostic."[24] Despite his nagging doubt, Darwin was committed to a materialist understanding of mankind's origin.

Design in the Aftermath of Darwin

Proponents of natural theology, including scientists, theologians, philosophers, and churchmen, had mixed reactions to Darwin's work. Some saw it as strictly a scientific theory about the *how* of creation that did nothing to undermine the *fact* of creation. They perceived no theological difficulty with the idea of secondary causation in the natural order. Others perceived evolutionary theory as an attempt to rule out divine creation or, at least, God's total sovereignty over nature. Those who viewed the theory as nonthreatening or even supportive of orthodox Christianity argued that "Darwin or design" represented a false dichotomy; they were not disturbed by the thought of God using natural causes in his creation of living things and believed that acceptance of Darwin's theory of common descent by way of natural selection did not require a materialist interpretation.

An excellent example of an eminent man of science who saw compatibility between Darwin's theory and design was Alfred Russel Wallace (1823–1913). Hailed as the co-discoverer of natural selection, Wallace was a scientific associate of Darwin who independently reached the same conclusions about the basic mechanism behind biological adaptation. Very much unlike Darwin, however, Wallace saw the evolutionary process as being infused with an "organizing and directive Life-Principle" by a "Creative Power" in order to achieve "ultimate Purpose":

> This Purpose, which alone throws light on many of the mysteries of its mode of evolution, I hold to be the development of man, the one crowning product of the whole cosmic process of life-development; the only being which can to some extent comprehend nature; which can perceive and trace out her modes of action; which can appreciate the hidden forces and motions everywhere at work, and can deduce from them a supreme and over-ruling Mind as their necessary cause.[25]

Here, Wallace emphasizes two main themes of the Maker Thesis by insisting that the evolutionary process does not preclude design, and by underscoring the fact that mankind is the pinnacle of creation, the only living being that has the rational capacity for scientific inquiry.

It is a fun quirk of history that a painted portrait of Alfred Russel Wallace now hangs beside one of Darwin at the prestigious Linnean Society, where the two men made their joint paper presentation on the theory of natural selection in 1858. It is another instance in which Darwin is, ironically, memorialized alongside of an advocate of intentional biological design.

Asa Gray (1810–1888), who corresponded with Darwin and was his most avid scientific supporter in the United States, specifically argued for the compatibility of natural theology (including the Palean design argument) and the theory of evolution by natural selection. Regarding Gray, an orthodox Christian of Presbyterian persuasion and a professor of botany at Harvard University, Darwin said, "No one person understands my views & has defended them so well as A. Gray;—though he does not by any means go all the way with me."[26] Gray, unlike Darwin, was convinced that natural selection did not diminish the potency of design argumentation. "We cannot doubt that the watch had a watchmaker," Gray argued, adding that an agent acting by secondary causation rather than immediate, supernatural intervention is nonetheless the mind wholly responsible for the contrivances of nature.[27]

Gray uses a cloth-making analogy to drive home his point, and the illustration is so reminiscent of Paley's that there can be little doubt that Gray had that passage from *Natural Theology* in mind when he wrote:

> Recall a woman of a past generation and show her a web of cloth; ask her how it was made, and she will say that the wool or cotton was carded, spun, and woven by hand. When you tell her it was not made by manual labor, that probably no hand has touched the materials throughout the process, it is possible that she might at first regard your statement as tantamount to the assertion that the cloth was made without design. If she did, she would not credit your statement. If you patiently explained to her

the theory of carding-machines, spinning-jennies, and power-looms, would her reception of your explanation weaken her conviction that the cloth was the result of design? It is certain that she would believe in design as firmly as before, and that this belief would be attended by a higher conception and reverent admiration of a wisdom, skill, and power greatly beyond anything she had previously conceived possible.[28]

For Gray, the fact that nature could be outfitted with a mechanism for adaptation and the descent of new species was reinforcement of design, not its destruction. He summed up his position by saying that "the argument for design, as presented by the natural theologians, is just as good now, if we accept Darwin's theory, as it was before that theory was promulgated."[29] He firmly believed that Paley's watchmaker argument is not at all weakened by supposing that "watches" are so designed to produce "better watches, and contrivances adapted to successive conditions."[30] In other words, creatures with the inherent ability to adapt to their environment and over time give rise to new species do nothing to rid themselves of the need for a designer. About the processes allegedly responsible for evolution, Gray said, "I shall not for one moment contend that these laws are incompatible with design and a self-conscious, intelligent creator."[31]

Significantly, Gray pointed out that Darwin's theory can do nothing to rule out intelligent design of life, because that is "a question which belongs to philosophy."[32] Whatever a person ultimately concludes about design in nature, the one thing that he or she cannot say is that the argument for design is weaker in the post-Darwin era. As for those who oppose the idea of evolution based on a belief that it undermined the doctrine of creation, Gray exclaimed, "How strange that a convinced theist should be so prone to associate design only with miracle!" In other words, gradual creation and instantaneous supernatural creation should, according to him, be seen as equally supportive of God's creative hand in nature.

The purpose behind citing scientific men who did not see a conflict between design and Darwinism is not to make any statement, one way or the other, on whether or not the theory of evolution by natural selection is true. Rather, it is simply meant to demonstrate the falsehood of the claim that Darwin's theory spelled the end for natural theology and was a decided victory for materialism. To be sure, Darwin's theory was, and still is, frequently used in an attempt to support the atheist worldview. One of Darwin's associates and most ardent supporters, Thomas Henry Huxley (a.k.a. "Darwin's Bulldog"), proclaimed that the idea of planning and purpose in nature "received its deathblow at Mr. Darwin's hands."[33] This sentiment has endured in some circles, but many others have realized that the theory does not require that philosophical interpretation. Historian of science John Hedley Brooke has pointed out that "scientific theories have usually been susceptible to both theistic and naturalistic readings."[34] As we have seen, evolutionary theory is a prime example.

In the decades following Darwin, natural theology—including design arguments—continued to have a noticeable presence in the writings of both proponents and opponents of evolutionary theory. Boston University professor of history Jon Roberts confirms that "even a cursory examination of the history of Christian thought in the Anglo-American world since 1859 is sufficient to indicate that natural theology remained an ongoing, sometimes even thriving, enterprise."[35] It is true, however, that the particular practice of arguing for design from the complexity of biological organisms did decline in popularity due to a wide range of complex sociological factors and theological debates that followed devastating world wars. This was actually a fortuitous turn of events in one particular respect: It encouraged natural theologians to explore additional scientific avenues, such as physics and cosmology, which turned out to be even more fruitful.

The Rise of Neo-Darwinism

In the mid-twentieth century, major leaps in molecular biology led to an understanding of how biological traits are inherited by each successive generation of living organisms. The blending of the new science of genetics with Darwin's theory of evolution by natural selection came to be known as *neo-Darwinism* ("new" Darwinism). Unfortunately, there is a lot of confusion about whether or not the terms "evolution," "neo-Darwinism," and "Darwinism" necessarily carry a materialist connotation. Different people use these terms in different ways, making the water very muddy. Since Darwin himself intended to establish a plausible account of design without supernatural guidance, it seems reasonable to reserve the use of his name for the idea that a Maker was in no way, shape, or form responsible for living things—a fully materialist view of natural history.

The basic term "evolution" seems most appropriate for the very general idea of common descent, that living things came about through a long history of biological change from one generation to the next. However, some evolutionary creationists tend to refer to their view as Darwinian, presumably to communicate their acceptance of the idea that once life first appeared on the scene, evolution—a process engineered and guided by God—did all the rest. Other evolutionary creationists go even further than this by claiming that God gave the material creation complete autonomy, allowing it to freely develop after the moment of the big bang, the moment when all the laws of nature were divinely established. In this latter view, there is a genuine element of randomness in life's history over which God did not exercise his sovereignty. The point is, it is not safe to assume what someone means when they use words like "evolution," "Darwinian," or "Darwinism." It is wise to always ask for clarification when such terms come up in conversation in order to avoid unnecessary disputes.

Today, those skeptical of theism often claim that a plausible account of an evolutionary descent of all life-forms gravely undercuts the case for a Maker. This chapter was intended to show that this is a *philosophical* inference, not a *scientific* one. Scientific evidence as such cannot rule out the intelligent engineering or even guidance of life's history.

In other words, we must not equate process with the elimination of agency, a fact that some of Darwin's scientific associates, such as William Paley and Asa Gray, pointed out well over a century ago. Whether or not life has any sort of evolutionary past, the Maker Thesis stands; moreover, we can attempt to make a positive case for it by examining the characteristics of life at the fundamental level to see if a theistic inference based upon biology is justified. This will be the focus of the next chapter.

Whether or not life has any sort of evolutionary past, the Maker Thesis stands.

Key Points

- Natural theology was a prominent characteristic of both natural philosophical (scientific) and theological writing in the English-speaking world in the eighteenth and nineteenth centuries.

- William Paley's famous watchmaker argument was based upon what he saw as "contrivances" in nature—parts that function in harmony for an intended purpose.

- An often overlooked fact is that Paley was aware of evolutionary speculations during his time and did not believe they threatened the design argument.

- Charles Darwin's theory of common descent by way of natural selection suggested a gradualistic mechanism by which to explain the complexity and diversity found in living organisms.

- Major scientific proponents of Darwinian theory, such as Alfred Russel Wallace (the co-discoverer of natural selection) and Asa Gray (a devout Christian), saw it as wholly compatible with (and even supportive of) arguments for design in nature.

- The discipline of natural theology began changing shape post-Darwin, but this was not, as some have assumed, because evolutionary theory discredited the project.
- Even if life has an evolutionary history, the Maker Thesis is not ruled out.

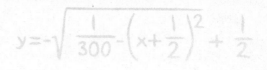

$$y=-\sqrt{\frac{1}{300}-\left(x+\frac{1}{2}\right)^2}+\frac{1}{2}$$

Chapter 7

The Language of Life:
The Marvels of DNA

Every time you understand something, religion becomes less likely. Only with the discovery of the double helix and the ensuing genetic revolution have we had grounds for thinking that the powers held traditionally to be the exclusive property of the gods might one day be ours.[1]

James Watson

As a scientist who's also a believer, the chance to uncover the incredible intricacies of God's creation is an occasion of worship. To be able to look, for the first time in human history, at all three billion letters of the human DNA—which I think of as God's language—it gives us just a tiny glimpse into the amazing creative power of his mind.[2]

Francis Collins

I t was 1953 when James Watson and Francis Crick proposed the double-helical structure of the DNA molecule, laying the foundation for modern molecular biology. Fifty years later, the Human Genome Project (HGP) published a map of the entire human genome; they called it the "blueprint for building a human being."[3] It is incredible that, in only a half century, knowledge about the instructions for the form and function of living organisms made such dramatic progress. Advancements included the discovery (first hypothesized by Crick in 1958) that DNA functions as a molecular code that translates to protein—the stuff of life. (Crick called this the "central dogma" of molecular biology.) Francis Collins, an evangelical Christian who served as one of the lead scientists of the HGP and the sixteenth director of the National Institutes of Health (NIH), has referred to the genetic code as "the language of God."

This chapter will explore how DNA points to the mind of a Maker. First, we will take a look at the structure of the DNA molecule and how the genome functions as a highly advanced, information-rich language. Armed with this basic understanding, we will then turn to origin-of-life research to see whether or not the emergence of genetic coding suggests that a designing Mind was involved. Finally, we will consider an argument for the design of life based upon the usefulness of biological systems (such as DNA) for creating or improving manmade technologies.

How Does DNA Work?

Most of us are familiar with a few facts about DNA (deoxyribonucleic acid). We recognize artistic renderings of the molecule; we know that every person has a unique DNA "fingerprint" that can be used to identify them and determine biological relationships; we understand that some diseases can be the result of genetic defects. But in order to appreciate how this wonderful molecule offers evidence for the mind of a Maker, it's necessary to know a bit more about its structure and function. Biochemistry is technical, to say the least, but throughout this section I will simplify the bare basics as much as possible. Don't worry if you don't track with every step; key points will be emphasized along the way to help you grasp the big picture.

The DNA molecule is a double helix, a shape that could be roughly described as a coiled ladder; the sides or "backbone" of the ladder are made up of molecules called *phosphates* and ring-shaped sugars called *ribose*. These phosphates and sugars are linked together in a sort of chain-like fashion, and these two chains run in opposite directions. Without going into the finer details, a good way to understand what is meant by "direction" is to imagine strands of alternating circular and triangular beads. If you had two identical strands of beads, you could place one beside the other in such a way that the triangular beads in one strand pointed up, and the triangular beads in the other strand pointed down. The constitution of the two strands is the same, but because of their geometry, it is possible for them to be in opposite orientation with respect to one another. The ends of the DNA sugar-phosphate chains are designated as 5' and 3'; the 5' end of one strand aligns with the 3' end of the other.

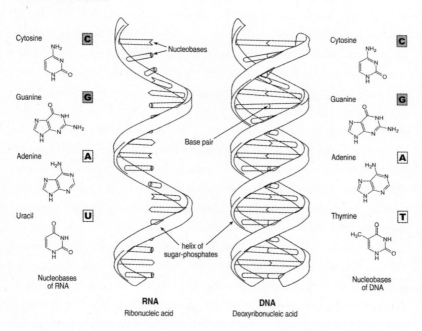

The rungs of the ladder that connect the two sugar-phosphate chains together are called *nucleotide base pairs*. There are four different bases: adenine (A), thymine (T), guanine (G), and cytosine (C). These bases are bonded on one side to one of the sugar-phosphate chains, and on the other side to a base that is bonded to the other chain. Adenine always bonds with thymine, and guanine always bonds with cytosine. So, for example, an A attached to one sugar-phosphate chain bonds with a T attached to the opposite chain, creating a base pair rung (see diagram). The sequence of the rungs from one end of the ladder to the other constitutes the digital genome of the organism, and this sequence contains segments of code in various lengths known as *genes*.

In a process known as *transcription*, the DNA molecule codes for a single-stranded complementary copy known as *mRNA* (m = messenger). The coding in the newly synthesized mRNA contains the bases A, C, and G, but uses a base called *uracil* (U) in the place of T. This transcription of DNA into mRNA is a finely orchestrated process involving all sorts of specialized protein structures that regulate and direct the biochemical dynamics. Once transcription is complete, the coding on the new mRNA molecule is used as the information for constructing the needed protein product. This process is known as *translation*, and it utilizes a cohort of other proteins and protein complexes. Simply put, the coding in the mRNA (which, remember, was determined by the coding in the DNA) dictates the order in which amino acids are bonded together into a long *polypeptide chain*. Once the chain is fully assembled, cell machinery helps it to fold into an intricate three-dimensional protein molecule based upon the order of its amino acids. At that point, gene expression is complete, and the shape of the brand new protein molecule determines the job it can perform.

The DNA, mRNA, and proteins in a living cell all exhibit something called *sequence specificity*. Sequence specificity is not mere complexity; it is a situation in which the precise arrangement of parts determines the function of the whole, in the same way that the arrangement of letters in a human language determines meaning in words and sentences. For example, consider the following string of characters:

kchate ut oth hovbsa eeardn sa pedli ermteru bebtr oc

This line of letters and spaces is complex, but it is gibberish; it doesn't contain meaningful information. However, if these same letters and spaces are arranged in a particular way—in a certain sequence— they *do* convey meaning:

like butter that has been scraped over too much bread[4]

This is analogous to the sequence specificity required in genetic coding. The sequence of the bases in the DNA molecule determines the sequence of bases in the mRNA copy, which in turn dictates the sequence of the amino acids in the polypeptide. Then the amino acid sequence determines the folding pattern of the polypeptide and thus the type of protein product. Without a highly specific sequence in the DNA, the polypeptides would not be able to fold correctly, and useful proteins would not be produced. Essentially, DNA provides the biological information for building the proteins necessary for constructing and running a living organism. DNA coding→mRNA coding→amino acid sequence in the polypeptide→functional protein.

In human cells, DNA is stored in threadlike structures called *chromosomes*, which are arranged in pairs inside the nucleus. Before one of our cells divides, it must generate a second batch of its chromosomes. DNA is a self-replicating molecule, but the replication process involves many biochemical helpers. When a cell is ready to divide into two identical "daughter" cells, a host of specialized proteins (themselves products of DNA coding) work together to unwind and separate the parent cell DNA, stabilize the strands, synthesize new complementary strands for each original strand, and rewind the two new molecules into double helices. Once the chromosomes in a cell have doubled, cellular division continues, resulting in two daughter cells that are genetically identical.

Taking all of this into account, the following questions arise: If living cells are constructed and operated by DNA, and new DNA comes from DNA replication, where did the *first* DNA molecule come from? In other words, how did the genetic information necessary for the first living cell come about?

Genetic Information and the Origin of Life

In his *Origin of Species*, Charles Darwin laid out his theory of how all living organisms that have ever lived descended from "one primordial form, into which life was first breathed."[5] Yet his book did not discuss the origin of this hypothetical first life-form, what modern evolutionary biologists refer to as the last universal common ancestor (LUCA). Darwin certainly pondered the problem of the origin of life; in a letter to Joseph Hooker dated February 1, 1871, he wrote:

> It is often said that all the conditions for the first production of a living organism are now present, which could ever have been present.— But if (& oh what a big if) we could conceive in some warm little pond with all sorts of ammonia & phosphoric salts,—light, heat, electricity [etc.] present, that a protein compound was chemically formed, ready to undergo still more complex changes, at the present day such matter would be instantly devoured, or absorbed, which would not have been the case before living creatures were formed.[6]

Darwin's concern was that the conditions on the earth during the time life allegedly arose in the primordial "soup" would have to have been quite different from modern conditions, which he believed to be too hostile for the chemical formation of an evolving, prebiotic molecule.

Today, origin-of-life researchers have much more information about earth's infancy, but are divided over the exact context in which this hypothesized chemical evolution of the first living microbes occurred. Some think that Darwin's "warm little pond" idea was pretty close to the truth—that geothermally heated waters of volcanic pools on Earth's surface would have contained high-enough concentrations of the necessary elements as well as the ultraviolet radiation exposure needed to spark the right chemical processes. Others believe that life arose around hydrothermal vents—areas on the ocean floor where magma and seawater converge. But regardless of environmental scenario, the central mystery to be solved in naturalistic accounts of the origin of life is the origin of genetic information, which is essential for cellular life and reproduction.

Darwin speculated that a simple protein compound could have formed and then evolved into the first life-form, but he (and all other scientists of his time) were completely ignorant of protein chemistry, DNA, and the relationship between the two. He was unaware of the sequence-specific genetic coding that is needed for manufacturing useful proteins within living cells. Modern researchers do understand the biochemistry, thus they are able to approach the problem at the most fundamental level—the origin of the biological information necessary for a self-replicating molecule that (they contend) could chemically evolve enough to get life started.

Although nailing down a definition for "life" is tricky, most would generally define a living organism as an entity that can absorb nutrients from its environment and process those nutrients into the energy necessary for growth and reproduction. Such activities, even in the simplest forms of life, require a highly complex information-processing system in which genetic information can be translated into all the necessary proteins. However, this system is itself made up of many key proteins. Similarly, DNA replication, which is an essential step in an organism's growth and reproduction, requires a protein infrastructure, yet all these proteins are manufactured based upon coding information in the DNA molecule. This creates a chicken-and-egg problem when it comes to the question of how life originated. Which came first, the DNA or the protein? Both the information stored in DNA *and* proteins capable of catalyzing certain biochemical processes are needed for life to get started. Even if (and "oh, what a big *if*," to quote Darwin) a segment of DNA containing a small amount of useful information could—against all odds—randomly form in the alleged primordial soup, that DNA fragment would be useless without the specialized proteins that facilitate information processing and replication. Similarly, a randomly formed simple protein molecule wouldn't be any good since it would not be able to self-replicate or code for DNA.

Because of these problems with the "DNA first" and "protein first" models, the currently popular origin-of-life hypothesis involves a prebiotic "RNA world" that would have come about by way of chemical evolution. This RNA world would have been populated with RNA molecules capable of carrying out functions of both DNA *and* proteins—self-replication and molecular assembly. The leading candidate for this multipurpose molecule is something called a *ribozyme*, which is an RNA molecule that carries information and catalyzes biochemical reactions. Unlike the ribozymes found in living organisms today, the hypothetical primordial ribozymes would have been self-replicators, which would have been required for evolution to gradually progress toward more complex molecules with a broader repertoire of functions. Proponents of the RNA world hypothesis argue that this self-replicating ribozyme would have eventually led to more complex molecules and then (by way of a diversity of other complex biochemical processes) the formation of the first living cells.

Is the RNA world scenario a reasonable theory for how life could have formed? Leaving aside the complete lack of evidence that a self-replicating ribozyme existed on the prebiotic earth, the question becomes this: How would such a complex molecule come about? It would have contained quite a lot of useful information in the specified complexity of its nucleotide base sequence in order to have the required functions. Before we consider the origin of this information, we must back up a step and ask whether or not the necessary building blocks for a ribozyme—nucleotide bases, ribose, and phosphates—would have been readily available. The situation doesn't look good. It turns out that in laboratory simulations of realistic prebiotic conditions, the formation and preservation of these building blocks has proven to be extremely difficult.[7] But suppose we simply grant, for the sake of the argument, that some spot on the early Earth contained all the necessary components. Is it scientifically feasible that the sequence specificity of a self-replicating ribozyme would arise by random, trial-and-error combinations of nucleotide bases? In other words, is it reasonable to believe that the necessary biological information would have emerged through mindless chemical processes?

In an attempt to demonstrate the plausibility of a fully naturalistic scenario, origin-of-life researchers perform experiments called *in vitro* (test tube) evolution—also known as *directed evolution*. The idea is that if the right RNAs can be made from scratch in the lab, then a chemical pathway by which this could have happened "in the wild" exists at least in principle. In stringently controlled laboratory setups (that, by the way, have not been shown to be reflective of the conditions likely on the early Earth), biochemists have had some limited success in synthesizing the right building blocks, prodding them into RNA chains, and then directing the evolution of this RNA into functional ribozymes. However, these experiments have (thus far) fallen short of producing the necessary type of self-replicating ribozymes.[8] Moreover, it should be noted that the biochemistry used in these laboratory procedures incorporates essential enzymes that would not have existed in the RNA world—a fact that is downplayed in popular-level discussions of origin-of-life studies.

> Scientists' attempts to identify possible pathways from dead chemicals to living cells reveal the crucial role of intelligent agents for even limited success in the laboratory.

Perhaps researchers will eventually succeed in artificially "evolving" the relevant RNA self-replicators in test tubes under realistic conditions, but what would this really show about a possible naturalistic path to life? During the extraordinarily tedious human-designed biochemistry protocols, intelligent researchers repeatedly intervene, fine-tuning the reaction conditions, manually halting certain phases before useful products would be destroyed, and selecting just the right chemicals and mineral substrates needed for the desired outcome.[9] The minds and hands of the researchers are vital in manipulating the experiments to make sure useful RNAs come together. This is the opposite of a demonstration that blind processes are a sufficient explanation for the origin of a first self-replicating molecule. In his book *Creating Life in the*

Lab, biochemist Fazale Rana explains, "If they prove anything more than the researchers' tenacity and ingenuity, efforts to provide experimental support for the RNA world scenario have demonstrated that life cannot 'happen' apart from the work of an intelligent, purposeful agent."[10] In other words, scientists' attempts to identify possible pathways from dead chemicals to living cells reveal the crucial role of intelligent agents for even limited success in the laboratory. This seems to represent positive evidence for the necessity of intelligence in the formation of the first life on earth.

Did Metabolism Come First?

Due to the seemingly intractable problems with the RNA world hypothesis, some researchers have abandoned it in favor of something called a *metabolism-first* origin-of-life scenario. The general idea is that once prebiotic molecules formed, they became organized into metabolic systems (systems that generate energy) that eventually became enclosed in membranes and evolved into the first truly living cells. Molecular self-replicators (DNA and RNA) would have somehow emerged later on. Metabolism-first models suffer from at least as many formidable problems as the RNA world; experimental support is very limited and chemical simulations of possible pathways require unrealistic conditions. In addition, it is doubtful that even simple forms of RNA or DNA could have evolved from metabolic systems.[11]

Leaving aside the fact that extensive agent manipulation in origin-of-life experiments highlights the necessity of intelligent intervention, any hypothetical breakthrough that outlined a workable scenario for the chemical evolution of a self-replicating molecule would not rule out the existence of a Maker. Think back to the previous chapter and the point made by Paley and Gray—that secondary causation does not rule out a creating Mind. In fact, everything that origin-of-life research-ers have learned to date has shown that many independent variables must align precisely to make any feasible pathway to a self-replicating molecule possible, such as having exactly the right environment at each successive stage of chemical evolution and all the needed molecular building blocks in proper concentrations. Such a finely tuned pro-cess suggests mindful orchestration. Moreover, it must be recognized that a self-replicating molecule is a *very* long way from an actual living cell with all its complex protein machinery and highly specific genetic coding.

Based upon knowledge gleaned through origin-of-life research, it would be sensible to conclude that there is a Mind whose intent was for living things to appear at a certain time in a certain place on earth. This is a philosophical inference based upon what we *know* about biochem-istry, not a gaps argument based upon the incompleteness of present theories. Given the evidence we have, we can ask which theory makes the most sense of it: goal-directed design or a blind chain of events. In light of what has been well established, the mindful design of life seems far more likely.

The Demise of "Junk" DNA

When scientists weigh the merits of a theory such as the natural-istic evolutionary origin of the human genome, one approach is to evaluate current evidence to see how well it fits the predictions of the theory. For example, some have argued that a genome that arose by blind, trial-and-error processes over eons of time would be expected to contain obvious evidence of such a messy history. It would likely con-tain regions of useless DNA sequence—so-called "junk" DNA—that accumulated through countless genetic mutations (copying mistakes) over the course of many generations. Indeed, genetic studies in the late twentieth century and early 2000s appeared to confirm the exis-tence of various types of seemingly superfluous DNA. It was discov-ered that only a tiny percentage of the human genome actually codes for protein products, and the assumption was that most of the rest was junk—dead remnants of the material processes that built it. Atheist Richard Dawkins remarked that "the greater part (95 per cent in the case of humans) of the genome might as well not be there, for all the difference it makes."[12]

Why would a mindful Maker create so much unnecessary sequence? That was the question advocates of intentional biological design had to face. In an article entitled "Life's Grand Design," biologist Kenneth Miller argued that the human genome is an excellent example of *un*intelligent design because obsolete stretches of DNA bear witness to an undirected evolutionary history. He said:

> If the DNA of a human being or any other organism resembled a carefully constructed computer program, with neatly arranged and logically structured modules each written to fulfill a specific function, the evidence of intelligent design would be overwhelming. In fact, the genome resembles nothing so much as a hodgepodge of borrowed, copied, mutated, and discarded sequences and commands that has been cobbled together by millions of years of trial and error against the relentless test of survival. It works, and it works brilliantly; not because of intelligent design, but because of the great blind power of natural selection to innovate, to test, and to discard what fails in favor of what succeeds.[13]

Miller's statement was reflective of the general consensus of the time. Many in the scientific community saw junk DNA as support for a materialist view of life's history. Richard Dawkins joked that "creationists might spend some earnest time speculating on why the Creator should bother to litter genomes with untranslated pseudogenes and junk tandem repeat DNA."[14]

The pseudogenes Dawkins mentioned are one category of (alleged) junk DNA. They are sequences that have the telltale biochemical features of genes yet seem to have no actual function. Sometimes they appear alongside an intact copy of the gene, suggesting that an original gene was duplicated at some point in evolutionary history, and then one of the copies became defunct because of random sequence mutations. The pseudogene copy, some believe, is simply a leftover "fossil." Dawkins's point was that the presence of such relics in the genome makes sense only in light of a naturalistic evolutionary process. Dawkins remarked, "What pseudogenes are useful for is embarrassing creationists. It stretches even their creative ingenuity to make up a convincing reason why an intelligent designer should have created a pseudogene—a gene that does absolutely nothing and gives every appearance of being...a gene that used to do something."[15]

In his 2006 book *The Language of God*, Francis Collins (an evolutionary creationist) highlighted a category of sequences called *ancient repetitive elements* (AREs) as an example of junk DNA. AREs, which include SINEs (short interspersed nuclear elements) and LINEs (long interspersed nuclear elements), are segments of DNA that copy and insert themselves in different locations in the genome. (Interestingly, comparable AREs tend to show up in similar locations in different species, such as humans and mice—a fact that is regarded by some as evidence for the common descent of mammals.) Collins argued that AREs are part of the "flotsam and jetsam" of our genetic makeup, since they seemed (at the time of his writing) to have no discernible function.[16] However, Collins did not see junk DNA as supportive of materialism, only as evidence for the method God used to create living things—a secondary process with a high degree of autonomy. (It is worth noting that some evolutionary creationists might see junk DNA as being consistent with a God-guided form of evolution; but for present purposes, we are concerned only with how junk DNA has been used to argue against the intelligent design of life.)

As knowledge of genome dynamics has increased over the past decade or so, the junk DNA narrative has collapsed like a house of cards. The landmark report that began shaking its foundation was released in 2012 by the ENCODE (Encyclopedia of DNA Elements) research project, whose mission is to compile a database of all the functional elements in the human genome. Initial data in phase one of their research (2007) had suggested that much of what had been classified as "junk" might indeed have functional significance; findings of the second phase of the project provided astounding confirmation. The ENCODE research team concluded that at least 80 percent of the genome has some kind of function—a shocking figure given the previous supposition that the nonprotein-coding regions, which make up approximately 98 percent of the genome, are useless.[17]

Research by ENCODE and others has shed important light on the purpose of sequences formerly known as junk DNA. For example, it turns out that some pseudogenes actually do code for proteins while some are transcribed to RNAs that, though not translated to proteins, still perform essential duties in the cell.[18] Granted, these represent only a fraction of all known pseudogenes, but further discoveries of pseudogene function are expected in light of what is now known. For example, it may be the case that some pseudogene RNA enhances the expression of the associated genes that *are* translated to proteins. Moreover, many repetitive DNA elements such as SINEs and LINEs are being shown to have functions such as the regulation of gene expression and cellular protection during physical stress.[19] It is also possible that SINEs help regulate embryonic development by controlling which genes are expressed during certain phases. We do know that LINEs play a crucial role in modulating the second X chromosome carried by females, which ensures an appropriate level of gene expression and prevention of genetic disorders.[20]

Although the function of a significant portion of noncoding DNA has yet to be nailed down, many researchers are now convinced that it must have an important role. They point to the fact that many different species of organisms share these noncoding sequences, and that if these sequences had no function, they would have degraded over time as the evolutionary tree branched into different species. What they have found instead is that these sequences have resisted the change that would come from the accumulation of DNA mutations. The bottom line is, the term "junk DNA" is now outmoded; as research continues, scientists are identifying essential functions for many of the sequences, and it seems that this trend will continue. This has arguably weakened the case for a naturalistic origin of the genome and strengthened the case for purposeful design.

If you've made it this far, congratulations, you've made it through the more difficult material in this chapter! As long as you got the gist of the preceding discussion, you're doing fine. What comes next is much less technical.

An Unrivaled Data Storage Medium

An amazing fact about the DNA molecule is that it is the most compact data storage medium in existence, far surpassing any man-made technology. Consider that the human genome contains over three billion base pairs arranged in specific sequences on strands of DNA. Two meters of DNA is tightly coiled into 23 pairs of chromosomes located within the nuclei of our cells—a space that is only 10 microns in diameter (a micron is one-millionth of a meter). The human body consists of around 10 trillion cells, which means it contains about 20 trillion meters of DNA—roughly 12.4 million miles! It is estimated that one gram of DNA—about the mass of a small paper clip—can be encoded with 215 million gigabytes of data. By way of comparison, that's the storage capacity of 4.3 million 50-gigabyte Blu-ray discs or several thousand of the densest computer hard drives available today. This means that all the data ever recorded by human beings throughout history could be encoded into a volume of DNA that would fit into a container roughly the size and weight of two pickup trucks.[21] DNA makes an outstanding storage medium; it is extremely stable at room temperature, unlike our current media, which degrade over time. In addition, it will never become obsolete; as long as there are human beings, technology for sequencing DNA will be available.

DNA: The Superior Software

In his book *River Out of Eden*, atheist Richard Dawkins directly compared DNA to engineered data storage:

> *Our genetic system, which is the universal system of all life on the planet, is digital to the core...Every cell in your body contains the equivalent of forty-six immense data tapes, reeling off digital characters via numerous reading heads working simultaneously. In every cell, these tapes—the chromosomes—contain the same information, but the reading heads in different kinds of cells seek out different parts of the database for their own specialist purposes...Life is just bytes and bytes and bytes of digital information. Genes are pure information—information that can be encoded, recoded, and decoded, without any degradation or change in meaning. Pure information can be copied and, since it is digital information, the fidelity of the copying can be immense. DNA characters are copied with an accuracy that rivals anything modern engineers can do.*[22]

Similarly, computer software giant Bill Gates has argued that DNA doesn't merely rival manmade technology, it dwarfs it. In his book *The Road Ahead*, Gates said that "DNA is like a computer program but far, far more advanced than any software we've ever created."[23]

For a few years, scientists have been experimenting with turning manmade information into DNA coding by designating the nucleotide base pairs (A-T and G-C) as either 1 or 0 (the binary code of computer data) and then artificially synthesizing DNA containing the desired sequence data. In one of the more recent projects, Yaniv Erlich, a Columbia University computer scientist, teamed up with Dina Zielinski, a scientist at the New York Genome Center, to convert six binary data files—including a complete computer operating system and an 1895 French film—into DNA coding. The coding was then sent to a biotechnology company in California that synthesized the actual DNA molecules. After Erlich and Zielinski received the vial of custom DNA in the mail, they used sequencing technology to read the sequence, then converted it to binary code and reassembled the original computer files. The new files turned out to be 100 percent faithful to the originals.[24] The success of this experiment confirmed DNA's suitability as an ultradense, high fidelity storage medium, one that far surpasses any media humans have yet been able to devise. This fact could eventually solve our looming human data storage crisis.

The fields of scientific research and engineering that look to biological designs for the invention and improvement of human technology are called *biomimetics* and *bioinspiration*. Biomimetics directly copies mechanisms from biology, whereas bioinspiration adapts biological design principles; both approaches have been used with very promising results. The experimental use of DNA as a data storage medium is a fine example of harnessing a design found in nature that far surpasses what even the most brilliant engineers have been able to develop.

The fact that biological systems are being used as models for the development of cutting-edge technology has interesting philosophical implications. Accordingly, Fazale Rana has developed an argument for the intelligent design of life based upon the growing success of biomimetics and bioinspiration; he calls it the "converse Watchmaker argument," a name that is a nod to the opening passage of William Paley's *Natural Theology*.[25] Rana explains, "If biological designs are the work of a Creator, then these systems should be so well-designed that they can serve as engineering models and, otherwise, inspire the development of new technologies."[26] He contends that the work being done in biomimetics and bioinspiration strongly implies that biological systems aren't simply *like* highly engineered artifacts of intelligence in important respects, they really *are* highly engineered artifacts.

If nature has a rational Mind as its ultimate source, it makes perfect sense for engineers to glean ideas from nature for solving problems and improving upon human technology. But if biological design arose through undirected processes as the materialist claims, then the success of biomimetics and bioinspiration research is quite unexpected. Rana says,

> [E]volutionary biologists view biological systems as the outworking of unguided, historically contingent processes that co-opt preexisting designs to cobble together new systems. Once these designs are in place, evolutionary mechanisms can optimize them, but even then they remain essentially kludges. If biological systems are, in effect, kludged together, why would engineers and technologists turn to them for inspiration? If produced by evolutionary processes—even if these processes operated over the course of millions of years—biological systems should make unreliable muses.[27]

If nature has a rational Mind as its ultimate source, it makes perfect sense for engineers to glean ideas from nature for solving problems and improving upon human technology.

Even if blind evolutionary processes have had eons to polish up biological systems through natural selection, those systems still wouldn't be expected to exhibit such a high level of elegance and sophistication. However, if a Mind is ultimately responsible for biological design, then it is not surprising that biology can provide models that aid technological advancement. Perhaps we could say that human engineers working in biomimetics and bioinspiration are, practically speaking, apprentices to the Maker.

Mimicking Designs from Nature

The practice of using nature as a guide for human inventions has been going on for centuries. For example, Leonardo da Vinci's conceptual drawings of flying machines (late fifteenth century) included a glider with birdlike wings. At the turn of the twentieth century, the Wright brothers' observation of birds in flight inspired the slightly arched wing shape of their aircraft. More recent examples of biomimicry include the Shinkansen bullet train in Japan, which has a beaklike structure on the front. Its design is inspired by the beaks of kingfishers, birds that are streamlined for diving through the air and water. The beaked train is more aerodynamic, making it energy efficient and quieter when going through tunnels. Geckos' toes, which have skin that allows them to cling to any surface, have inspired specialized silicone used in several inventions, such as a device for climbing vertical glass surfaces. Solar cells have been developed that mimic the energy-production process of plant photosynthesis, and wind turbine blades have been modeled off of the bumpy fins of humpback whales. Time and again, designs in nature have enabled engineers to significantly improve human technology.

DNA and the Maker Thesis

In sum, DNA, which contains a complex translatable code, strongly suggests that a Mind is responsible for the design of living things. Origin-of-life research has emphasized the need for intelligent guidance in the formation of even the basic building blocks necessary for the construction of these information-rich molecules. Moreover, DNA's vast superiority as a storage medium is quite peculiar if it was not mindfully intended for that purpose. The more we learn, the more ingenious the language of life turns out to be.

It is also quite interesting that the genome functions in a rational manner that is analogous to human language, a fact that facilitates scientific insight. We might infer from this conspicuous comprehensibility that the design of life was meant to be illuminated by human scientists. In addition, it seems unreasonable to expect that minds which have, allegedly, evolved by natural selection to be fit for survival and reproduction would be suitably equipped to grasp the complexities of molecular biology, much less harness its principles for high-tech engineering purposes. Perhaps the best explanation for this situation is that human minds—unlike any others—have a peculiar resonance with the mind of the Maker.

Key Points

- The discovery of the structure of the DNA molecule gave rise to modern molecular biology.

- The sequence of the bases in DNA constitutes an organism's genetic code, instructions that are necessary for the development and function of a living organism.

- Origin-of-life research has highlighted the importance of intelligence in the formation of self-replicating molecules, which are foundational to living cells.

- The junk DNA argument is all but obsolete; researchers continue to discover function for noncoding sequences.

- Biomimicry and bioinspiration lend support to what Fazale Rana calls the converse Watchmaker argument—the idea that designs in nature can serve as models for engineering because those designs are themselves mindfully engineered.

Chapter 8

Revival of the God Hypothesis: Twentieth-Century Physics and Cosmology

There are two ways of getting home; and one of them is to stay there. The other is to walk round the whole world till we come back to the same place.[1]

G.K. Chesterton

During the first several decades of the twentieth century, the disciplines of physics and cosmology enjoyed major advancements that provided new insights into the nature and origin of the universe. This set the stage for important developments in the science and theology conversation, including a renewed emphasis upon what we have observed as one of natural theology's oldest and most resilient roots: the rationality of the cosmos and its transparency to the intellect of man. In this way, twentieth-century physics and cosmology reinforced the reasons scientists of the scientific revolution believed that the mind of God was plainly manifest in nature.

This chapter will profile the main scientific achievements and the philosophical writings of three celebrated scientists whose insights about nature and mankind serve as valuable support for the Maker Thesis: Max Planck, Albert Einstein, and Arthur Eddington. Though not all of these were religious believers in the ordinary sense, they did not refrain from discussing the philosophical or theological implications they drew from their growing understanding of the universe.

A New Revolution

We begin with Max Planck (1858–1947), a German theoretical physicist at the University of Berlin. It was the year 1900 when Planck developed the theory that earned him the 1918 Nobel Prize and remembrance as the father of quantum theory—the field of physics dealing with how matter and energy behave at the atomic and subatomic levels. Planck theorized that energy exists in individual units—*quanta*—instead of continuous waves. He came up with a mathematical equation that could be used to represent the relationship between the energy of a photon (a quantum) and its frequency.[2] Planck's work demonstrated that the established laws of classical physics do not apply at such a tiny scale, and our understanding of physical reality at the fundamental level was forever changed. As a result, the field of quantum mechanics was born.

Planck regarded science and faith as compatible and complementary enterprises. He was particularly fascinated by the congruence between the mathematical, law-governed structure of the material world and human rationality; he saw this correspondence as indicative of a designing Mind. During the last decade of his life, he wrote a series of essays that went on to be published (posthumously, in 1949) in English under the title *Scientific Autobiography and Other Papers*. The first essay in the collection, "Scientific Autobiography," opens with the following pronouncement:

> My original decision to devote myself to science was a direct result of the discovery which has never ceased to fill me with enthusiasm since my early youth—the comprehension of the far from obvious fact that the laws of human reasoning coincide with the laws governing the sequences of the impressions we receive from the world about us; that, therefore, pure reasoning can enable man to gain an insight into the mechanism of the latter.[3]

Planck recognized the remarkable, "far from obvious fact" that the human intellect is suited for scientific discovery. Like so many others before and since, he pondered why there should be such a happy resonance between the fundamental workings of nature and the mind of man.

In the final essay of the collection, which is entitled "Religion and Natural Science," Planck set forth an updated expression of the persistent ideas about detectable design in nature and man's relationship to both creation and the Creator. He remarked that the world is "ruled by definite laws which are independent of the existence of thinking human beings; but these laws, insofar as they can all be comprehended by our senses, can be given a formulation which is adapted for purposeful activity"—in other words, nature is ordered in such a way that it is accessible through the (mathematical) scientific enterprise.[4] Again, Planck expressed amazement at man's scientific aptitude:

> How pitifully small, how powerless we human beings must appear to ourselves if we stop to think that the planet Earth on which we live our lives is just a minute, infinitesimal mote of dust; on the other hand how peculiar it must seem that we, tiny creatures on a tiny planet, are nevertheless capable of knowing though not the essence at least the existence and dimensions of the basic building blocks of the entire great Cosmos![5]

Planck went on to articulate his expectation that the progress of the natural sciences would advance mankind's insights about "the omnipotent Reason which rules over Nature"; he argued that the God of religion is "the power acting in accordance with natural laws for which the sense data of the scientist provide a certain degree of evidence" and that "both religion and natural science require a belief in God for their activities."[6] In claiming that natural science requires "belief in God," he seems to mean that the sciences require certain major assumptions that theism explains: that the physical world is rationally ordered and that man is mentally capable of elucidating that order. Moreover, he explained that there is great harmony between theism and the natural sciences—that they have the common goal of illuminating reality, and that the ultimate truth toward which these parallel streams are flowing is God. He described the joint battle of science and religion as a pursuit of knowledge and crusade against both skepticism and dogmatism. He ended the essay with the rallying cry, "On to God!"[7]

Enter: Einstein

Arguably the most important theoretical physicist of the twentieth century and considered the father of modern physics, Albert Einstein (1879–1955) is a valuable part of the Maker Thesis discussion. Einstein believed that the materialist view of nature is inadequate for explaining why we live in a universe that is fundamentally mathematical and therefore comprehensible to the human scientist. In his own way, he saw divinity in the natural order; he sensed that there was something more to the world than matter in motion.

Einstein is best known for his theories of special and general relativity, which transformed the scientific understanding of space, time, and gravity. His name has become practically synonymous with "genius," and most everyone recognizes his famous equation, $E=mc^2$. In 1905, Einstein proposed his theory of special relativity, which revealed the very weird fact that time slows down at a rate relative to an object's acceleration through space, and would (theoretically) stop altogether if the object reached light speed.[8]

After serving as a university professor in Zurich and Prague, Einstein accepted an invitation to join Max Planck (who had been impressed by Einstein's paper on special relativity) and an elite group of scientists at the University of Berlin in 1914. It was there, in 1915, after a period of painstaking and frustrating labor over the mathematical equations, that Einstein presented another groundbreaking paper, "The Foundation of the General Theory of Relativity" (published in early 1916). As mentioned in an earlier chapter, these equations (once empirically confirmed) overthrew the Newtonian conception of gravity by showing that the curvature of space-time around objects—rather than a pulling force *exerted* by objects—is responsible for gravitation. In 1922, Einstein received the Nobel Prize for physics (for the previous year), chiefly for his discovery of the photoelectric effect—the dislodging of an electron from a metal surface when a high-energy light photon collides with it. This work served as a foundation for the emerging field of quantum mechanics; the irony was, the mathematical theory of quantum mechanics conflicted with the theory of general relativity. Einstein was convinced that nature is a coherent whole, and his ultimate goal in theoretical physics was a theory that unified and harmonized the two theories. This goal was never realized and remains the holy grail of theoretical physics.

An international celebrity of science by his forties, Einstein was a highly visible participant in the public science and theology conversation. Although he clearly rejected organized religion as well as all conceptions of a personal deity involved with human affairs, he often made enigmatic statements about his beliefs regarding the existence and nature of God, and these have been interpreted in different ways. He has been categorized by some scholars as a pantheist, which is (generally speaking) a person who identifies God with the material cosmos itself. However, Einstein seems to have been dissatisfied with this characterization of his religious views. "I'm not an atheist, and I don't think I can call myself a pantheist," he said, while at other times he expressed what he called an "admiration" for Spinozan pantheism (the view of Baruch Spinoza, a seventeenth-century Dutch philosopher) or even claimed "Spinoza's god" as his own.[9] Perhaps a better way to describe Einstein's conception of God would be deism with a marked pantheistic bent.

Despite the uncertainty regarding the appropriate way to label his view on God, it is indisputable that Einstein perceived a kind of inscrutable divinity in the mathematical organization of the universe and found it remarkable that human beings have the capacity to comprehend even a small part of it:

We are in the position of a little child entering a huge library filled with books in many languages...The child dimly suspects a mysterious order in the arrangement of the books but doesn't know what it is. That, it seems to me, is the attitude of even the most intelligent human being toward God. We see the universe marvelously arranged and obeying certain laws but only dimly understand these laws. Our limited minds grasp the mysterious force that moves the constellations.[10]

It's interesting that he would use imagery—a book-filled library—that comes so close to the book of nature metaphor. Einstein admitted to having a deep religiosity characterized by "a humble admiration of the infinitely superior spirit who reveals himself in the slight details we are able to perceive with our frail and feeble minds."[11] In several of his writings he spoke of his "rapturous amazement at the harmony of natural law, which reveals an intelligence of such superiority that, compared with it, all systematic thinking and acting of human beings is an utterly insignificant reflection."[12]

Einstein more explicitly mentioned the themes of a rationally structured universe and its correspondence with the human mind in a series of letters to Romanian philosopher and mathematician Maurice Solovine, in which he said, "I have never found a better expression than 'religious' for this trust in the rational nature of reality and of its peculiar accessibility to the human mind."[13] He was careful to distinguish between the idea of the human mind *imposing* order on the cosmos and *discovering* order within it:

Well, *a priori* one should expect a chaotic world which cannot be grasped by the mind in any way. One could (yes *one should*) expect the world to be subjected to law only to the extent that we order it through our intelligence. Ordering of this kind would be like the alphabetical ordering of the words of a language. By contrast, the kind of order created by Newton's theory of gravitation, for instance, is wholly different. Even if the axioms of the theory are proposed by man, the success of such a project presupposes a high degree of ordering of the objective world, and this could not be expected *a priori*. That is the "miracle" which is being constantly reinforced as our knowledge expands.[14]

Einstein rightly highlights the fact that there is no reason to expect the universe to be arranged in a way that the human intellect can grasp. Moreover, he insists that even if human scientists devised the mathematical starting point from which to investigate, an amazing degree of orderliness must be inherent to the universe for this type of mathematical research to even be possible.

It is important to understand that Einstein's views about religion were at least partially influenced by his philosophy of nature. He believed the world to be a closed material system that operates according to deterministic processes. In other words, nothing or no one can miraculously intervene in the physical order from the "outside," the way the God of monotheism is purported to do. Therefore, any religion that involved miracles was, for him, untenable. He included brain chemistry in his deterministic view, thereby denying that human beings have authentic free will. This explains why he was staunchly opposed to the notion of divine reward and punishment—neither could be deserved if a person's behavior is merely the result of physics, chemistry, and the impact of his or her environment, if he or she is nothing more than the sum of his or her physical parts. (Later, we will see why Einstein's unwavering commitment to physical determinism was incompatible with his beliefs about the rational foundation of science.) To his credit, he did admit that there is truth in the adage "the man of science is a poor philosopher." But, as we have seen, this did not deter him from quite a bit of philosophizing.[15]

Eddington on the Cosmic Origin, Mathematics, and Mind

Regarded as the father of modern theoretical astrophysics, Sir

Arthur Eddington (1882–1944) contributed much more to twentieth-century science than the eclipse photographs that confirmed Einstein's theory of general relativity. One of Eddington's great fascinations was the movements of the stars, and his first book, *Stellar Movements and the Structure of the Universe*, established him as the founder of the discipline of stellar dynamics. He went on to develop a theory of how stars evolved, but turned his attention to the study of relativity theory after his 1919 expedition to Africa provided the key observational data. He then wrote what Einstein declared to be the best treatment of relativity: *The Mathematical Theory of Relativity*.

Eddington was born, raised, and remained a Quaker until his death. As such, he was an outlier in the world of England's intellectual elite, which at the time was almost synonymous with "Anglican elite."[16] Concerning the intersection of science and theology, Eddington rejected the idea that scientific evidence could be used as proof for the existence and attributes of God. He did, however, have quite a lot to say about the philosophical and theological implications of science. This included his ideas about the origin of the universe and what science is (or is not) able to reveal about it, the usefulness of mathematics in the sciences, and the question of human nature (the kind of thing man is).

In *The Expanding Universe*, a popular-level book that explained the theory of origins developed by Lemaître (recall Lemaître's "primeval atom"), Eddington acknowledged that the birth of the expanding universe from some first primordial state meant there must have been a cause for such an event, what he called "an ultimate beginning."[17] He cautioned that such questions "lie almost beyond scientific argument" because science cannot give us "reasons why the world should have been created one way rather than another."[18] Eddington was open about being opposed to the idea of an abrupt, explosive origin—Lemaître's "fireworks theory" (later known as big bang theory)—and suggested instead: "an even distribution of protons and electrons, extremely diffuse and filling all (spherical) space, remaining nearly balanced for an exceedingly long time until its inherent instability prevails... There is no hurry for anything to begin to happen. But at last small irregular tendencies accumulate, and evolution gets under way."[19]

Eddington suggested that particles in this primordial physical reality could have begun condensing and then the evolution of stars, complex elements, planets, and then life would have followed. He admitted that this didn't answer the question of the ultimate origin of things, but then he tried to do an end run around that problem by saying that, to his mind, "*undifferentiated sameness* and *nothingness* cannot be distinguished philosophically." To those who might remain dissatisfied with his theory, he said, "Have it your own way. And now let us get away from the Creation back to problems that we may possibly know something about."[20]

At the end of the book, Eddington briefly revisited this conundrum of origins. He said, "The beginning seems to present insuperable difficulties unless we agree to look on it as frankly supernatural. We may have to let it go at that."[21] He noted that scientific investigation can back the problem up a step or two, but eventually reaches a barrier beyond which it cannot proceed. "Perhaps," he said, "it is this barrier that we call 'the beginning.'"[22]

The dramatic advancements being made in physics and astrophysics during the decades of Eddington's career placed unprecedented emphasis upon a key observation: that mathematics functions as a tool for scientific discovery. He was so impressed by the utility of mathematical equations in astrophysics that he often made remarks to that effect in his writing. For example, in *The Expanding Universe*, he discussed how astrophysicists determine the rate at which spiral nebulae (what we now call "spiral galaxies") are receding from the earthly observer's perspective: by combining the mathematical equations of quantum theory and those used in wave mechanics. "By combining the two theories," he explained, "we can make the desired theoretical calculation of the speed of recession"; he gave the mathematical range in which this speed falls and then added, "No astronomical observations of any kind are used in this calculation, all the data being found in the laboratory. Therefore when we turn our telescopes and spectroscopes on the distant nebulae and find them to be receding at a speed within these limits the confirmation is striking."[23] Confidence in the precision with which these equations describe nature (even when observational confirmation is not available) is enhanced by the fact that they are applicable to more than one question for which physical measurements can corroborate the mathematical results; "there is an artistry in these fundamental equations of physics which one cannot trifle with," said Eddington.[24] He expressed his desire to show his readers "that all the necessary physical ideas present themselves naturally, and are waiting for the mathematician to express them in symbols and work out the answer."[25]

Though his area of scientific expertise did not include the study of human nature, Eddington realized that one's philosophy of physics has a bearing on one's understanding of the kind of thing a human being is. He accepted the evolutionary account of mankind's biological origin, but insisted that the physical body is not all there is to human nature, and that (contrary to the claims of Einstein and others) we are not puppets of deterministic material processes. Thus he saw consciousness as a major point in favor of a dualistic understanding of man (body plus soul/spirit), and as a phenomenon which a comprehensive understanding of the material world would still exclude. The question then becomes how to explain the interaction of the mental and the physical:

> Hence arises insistently the problem of the dualism of spirit and matter. On the one side there is consciousness stirring with activity of thought and sensation; on the other side there is a material brain, a maelstrom of scurrying atoms and electric charges. Incommensurable as they are, there is some kind of overlap or contact between them.[26]

Though physics can mathematically describe the dynamics of the "cogs and wheels" of brain activity, it is barred from similarly explaining our first-person mental experience.

In terms of the conscious willing of bodily movement (a perfect example of the overlap between mind and body that he mentions here), Eddington describes it as a correlation between thoughts in the mind and the atoms of the brain that initiate nerve impulses leading to muscle movement. He contrasts his view with what he calls the "most crudely materialistic view" of the mind-brain relationship, the idea "that the dance of atoms in the brain really constitutes the thought, that in our search for reality we should replace the thinking mind by a system of physical objects and forces, and that by so doing we strip away an illusory part of our experience and reveal the essential truth which it so strangely disguises."[27] In other words, if the mind is just the material brain itself, we are not truly the masters of our thoughts or will; we just think we are.

Another reason Eddington offered for understanding the brain and the mind as two fundamentally different entities is the fact that physical systems adhere to natural laws and cannot break those laws, whereas mental processes often fail to adhere to the laws of logic, the rules for "the way our minds ought to think." For physical mechanisms, how operation ought to occur and how it does occur are identical; but in mental activity, how we *ought* to think isn't always how we *do* think. Our conscious thoughts, unlike our material brain processes, have informational content over which we deliberate to draw true or false conclusions. Eddington argued, "However closely we may associate thought with the physical machinery of the brain, the connection is dropped as irrelevant as soon as we consider the fundamental property of thought—that it may be correct or incorrect."[28] For instance, we can make a mistake in reasoning through a math equation, but it makes no sense to say that the movements of the atoms in the brain broke any sort of law. "Dismiss the idea that natural law may swallow up religion; it cannot even tackle the multiplication table single-handed," Eddington quipped. He saw that true rationality, defined as processing received facts according to the immaterial laws of logic, is impossible on the materialist view, in which brains do what they do inevitably, according to the laws of physics.

What occurs in the brain during conscious reasoning might be fully described scientifically, but that's only part of the explanation. Eddington gave an excellent illustration to make this point. He suggested imagining a group of scientifically inclined aliens visiting England to study sound phenomena. They arrive on Armistice Day, during which all citizens simultaneously participate in two minutes of memorial silence, but these aliens know nothing whatsoever about this holiday and its traditions. As the aliens are observing and analyzing the roar of traffic and the sounds of other human activity, there is a sudden pause in which all sound ceases, and there is utter stillness for a period of two minutes before all the commotion abruptly begins again. The extraterrestrial scientists would be able to give a full account of all the natural forces at work; they would determine that "[t]he noise ceased because the traffic stopped; each car stopped because a brake applied the necessary friction; the brake was worked mechanically by a pedal; the pedal by a foot; the foot by a muscle; the muscle by mechanical or electrical impulses travelling along a nerve."[29] Yet this physical understanding of deterministic cause and effect would not explain *why* there were two minutes of silence because that has to do with the informational content of the thoughts of the humans involved—what Eddington called the significance of the silence. He said, "The more complete the scientific explanation of the silence the more irrelevant that explanation becomes to our experience."[30]

· · · · · · · ·

The grand achievements of twentieth-century physics and cosmology highlight three facts great scientists of preceding centuries saw as evidence for the Maker Thesis: (1) the laws of nature are mathematical, (2) mathematics facilitates scientific discovery, and (3) the corresponding higher rational faculties of mankind make science possible. In addition, some scientists, such as Arthur Eddington, drew attention to the problem human rationality poses for the materialist worldview. As we shall see, these ideas remain highly relevant in contemporary discussions about whether or not there is a rational Mind behind the mathematically intelligible cosmos—a Mind in whose image we are made.

Key Points

- The enormous advancements of physics in the twentieth century gave fresh support and significance to the centuries-old observation that the laws of nature are written in the language of mathematics; for some scientists, this was striking evidence of a rationality behind nature.

- Max Planck believed that science and religion are compatible enterprises. He saw the congruence between the mathematical, law-governed structure of the material world and human rationality as striking evidence for the mind of the Maker.

- Albert Einstein, whose theories of special and general relativity revolutionized our understanding of gravitation and space-time, saw divinity in the orderliness of nature.

- Arthur Eddington, like Einstein, disliked the fact that physics seemed to rule out a past-eternal universe, and he proposed a speculative alternative.

- Eddington believed that human beings are more than just their physical bodies, and that the mind (or soul) is not subject to deterministic physical processes.

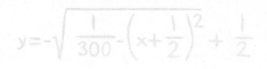

$$y = -\sqrt{\frac{1}{300} - \left(x + \frac{1}{2}\right)^2} + \frac{1}{2}$$

Chapter 9

A Meeting of the Minds: Our Comprehensible Mathematical Universe

Neither has it been without reason numbered among God's praises, "Thou hast ordered all things in number, and measure, and weight."[1]

St. Augustine

Philosophy is written in this all-encompassing book that is constantly open before our eyes, that is the universe; but it cannot be understood unless one first learns to understand the language and knows the characters in which it is written. It is written in mathematical language.[2]

Galileo Galilei

I must have been six or seven years old when my parents got rid of the rabbit-ears antennae on our wooden console cabinet television and subscribed to the local cable service. I still remember the rapturous wonder I felt upon discovering the phenomenon known as the Disney Channel. In the 1980s, the programming consisted of everything we now know as classic Disney (wow, I feel old), including a rotating assortment of animated shorts and films featuring the iconic animal characters. One that was shown periodically was the 1959 production entitled *Donald in Mathmagic Land*, which introduced me to the ideas of the Pythagoreans—ancient Greeks who saw numbers as the very essence of the natural world. I was mesmerized by the visual demonstrations of the fact that both the natural world and great human art exhibit shapes, symmetries, harmonies, and proportions that are thoroughly mathematical. In the film, the beautiful logarithmic spiral of the nautilus shell and the pentagonal geometry of various flowers and marine life are shown as examples of how mathematical patterns abound in nature.

While rewatching it not long ago, I happily noticed that *Donald in Mathmagic Land* illustrates the subtle connections between the mathematical qualities of nature, the usefulness of mathematics in the sciences, and the mind of a Maker. After the fascinating visual and musical examples of how mathematics pervades the world, the narrator says, "Mathematical thinking has opened the doors to the exciting adventures of science," and then the film ends with Galileo's famous statement about mathematics being the language in which God has written the universe. The implication, deliberate or not, is that the mathematical qualities of the physical world that allow mankind to carry out scientific activity are evidence of an intelligent Creator.

This chapter will explore the extraordinary resonance between the order of the cosmos, mathematics, and the corresponding faculties of the human mind. This three-part harmony is an advantageous arrangement that makes the natural sciences possible and invites serious philosophical reflection. Why is it that numbers and their complex operations relate to the material world with incredible precision? Some materialists insist that there is nothing at all exceptional about mathematics working so well in driving scientific discovery, because it is simply a case of a manmade system of abstract equations being devised to describe natural phenomena.

But is this true? Is mathematics merely a number game that has been created by the human mind for application to the material world, like sewing a glove to fit a specific hand? Or rather, is it something that transcends nature and—for some very mysterious reason—provides the most powerful tools known to science? Could it be, as the Maker Thesis claims, that human rationality, objective mathematical truths, and the material realm have a common, rational source—a Mind who intended the prodigious success of the natural sciences?

Mathematics: Invented or Discovered?

In order to properly explore these questions, it is helpful to begin with a consideration of the nature of mathematical truths. Intuitively, it seems right to say that they are objectively and timelessly true even if no humans existed to be aware of them. For instance, in a universe devoid of rational creatures, it would still be the case in standard arithmetic that ten divided by five is two and that the interior angles of a triangle add up to 180 degrees in Euclidean geometry.

> Intuitively, it seems right to say that mathematical truths are objectively and timelessly true even if no humans existed to be aware of them.

Several eminent thinkers have convincingly argued that we discover, rather than invent, the realities of mathematics. In his book *Principles of Mathematics*, renowned atheist philosopher and mathematician Bertrand Russell (1872–1970) said, "Arithmetic must be discovered in just the same sense in which Columbus discovered the West Indies, and we no more create numbers than he created the Indians [indigenous people of the Caribbean]."[3] In his famous work *A Mathematician's Apology*, English mathematician G.H. Hardy (1877–1947) also argued for the independent existence of mathematical truths:

> For me, and I suppose for most mathematicians, there is another reality, which I will call "mathematical reality"…Some hold that it is "mental" and that in some sense we construct it, others that it is outside and independent of us. A man who could give a convincing account of mathematical reality would have solved very many of the most difficult problems of metaphysics. If he could include physical reality in his account, he would have

> solved them all...I believe that mathematical reality lies
> outside us, that our function is to discover or observe it,
> and that the theorems which we prove, and which we
> describe grandiloquently as our "creations," are simply our
> notes of our observations.[4]

It is quite striking that Hardy calls explaining the existence of mathematical reality a difficult problem of *metaphysics* (meaning "beyond
physics"), which is outside the scope of scientific investigation. This
being the case, objective mathematical truth poses a problem for a strict
materialist philosophy, which denies that there is any reality independent of matter and energy.

Roger Penrose, a secular humanist and one of the world's leading
mathematical physicists, agrees with Russell and Hardy's assessment.[5]
Penrose is a modern-day Platonist, convinced that there is an abstract
realm of mathematical truth that is self-existent rather than the product of human thought. Regarding mathematics (in light of his own scientific research) he says,

> I couldn't have known what to do in a certain sense if
> the mathematics hadn't already *been* there. It's not us that
> impose this on the world, it's *out there*...I like to think of
> mathematics as a bit like archaeology or geology where
> you're really exploring something out there in the world,
> and you're finding beautiful things, things which have
> been there for ages and ages and ages, and you're revealing
> them for the first time.[6]

Penrose recognizes the timeless objectivity of mathematics, which, fortunately for scientists, is there for the taking. He says, "Sometimes people think that maybe the reason we have good mathematical laws of
physics is that that's the best way we can come to understand the world;
but it's something more than that."[7]

Note that it is necessary to make a distinction between the *language*
of mathematics (which is indeed invented) with the *conceptual truths*

of mathematics. For instance, consider the set of three-dimensional shapes known as the "Platonic solids," all the geometrical solids that are each composed of all identical sides—the tetrahedron, octahedron, hexahedron, dodecahedron, and icosahedron (see diagram). These are not inventions of the human mind; rational aliens in another part of the universe could discover this exact five-member set, only they would use a different language to describe these solids. Their set would contain all and only the exact same members as what we here on Earth call the set of Platonic solids. The aliens would not be free to invent a sixth one because no such shape exists.[8]

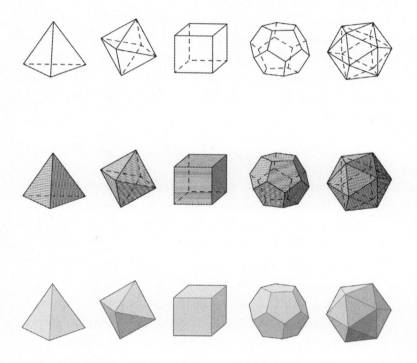

The same could be said about the relationships between numbers. For instance, we say three plus two equals five, and though the rational aliens would use different terms, they would have the concepts of what we might describe as "three-ness," "two-ness," and "five-ness," as well as that of addition. The aliens might use different words, but the ideas would be fundamentally the same. Thus it makes more sense to say that rather than being made up, abstract mathematical truths are part of a higher reality that is accessed through reason. This is why mathematics can function as a universal language.

The Unreasonable Effectiveness of Mathematics

In 1960, Hungarian physicist Eugene Wigner (1902–1995) published what would become a classic essay on the mysterious fact that mathematics can be used to investigate nature: "The Unreasonable Effectiveness of Mathematics in the Natural World." In his essay, Wigner discussed the astounding degree to which mathematics maps on to the material world; he explained that "mathematical concepts turn up in entirely unexpected connections...they often permit an unexpectedly close and accurate description of the phenomena in these connections."[9]

Eugene Wigner, Friendly Agnostic

Sent to a technical institute to study chemical engineering for the benefit of the family leather tanning business, Eugene Wigner was destined for a far more illustrious future. He was keenly interested in the work of Einstein, Planck, and other scientists involved with the emerging field of quantum theory, and invested six decades in the study of crystals, molecules, atoms, and atomic nuclei. He was a highly celebrated scientist, winning many awards, such as the Max Planck Medal in 1961, the Nobel Prize for Physics in 1963, and the National Medal of Science in 1969. He is also known for his work designing nuclear reactors for the US government during World War II.

Wigner came from a nominally Jewish family, but, like Einstein, much of his childhood education occurred in a Christian school (Lutheran, specifically). While he was still a boy, Communism came to power in Hungary, and Wigner's father was very disturbed by the fact that some of the movement's leaders were Jewish. In response to this, their entire family entered the Lutheran church, but Wigner never developed much of a personal religiosity. Though he lacked any true conviction about the reality of God, he maintained a gracious attitude toward those who believed, and he did not entirely avoid church. In the autobiography he dictated near the end of his life, he remarked, "Today, I am only mildly religious. When I attend church, it is with the Protestants."[10] Throughout his adult life, he found common science-related arguments for the existence of God unsatisfactory, and recalls how he replied to those who had spoken of God creating the earth: "Well, how had He made it? With an earth-making machine?"[11]

Wigner offered a nice illustration to help readers understand why this is an unexpected state of affairs. Imagine that you need to open a long succession of locked doors. For that purpose, you are given a large key ring with many unlabeled keys attached. You approach the first door, and the first key you try opens the door. At the second door, you randomly select a different key, and *it* works. As you move down the hallway, you find that you're able to open each door on either the first or second try by indiscriminately selecting one of the keys. You would, said Wigner, soon become skeptical that the keys were each uniquely paired with a specific door, and would suspect that many of the locks and keys were of the same design. In a similar way, the tools of mathematics are suited to questions in physics with an uncanny frequency and precision. "The enormous usefulness of mathematics in the natural sciences is something bordering on the mysterious," said Wigner, "there is no rational explanation for it."[12]

Compounding this strangeness is the fact that it is often the case that complex mathematical systems that were developed independently of any thought about possible physical application later turn out to be exceptionally useful in the physical sciences, much like a lock-and-key fit. To extend Wigner's analogy, this would be like manufacturing an intricately shaped key simply for the sake of the beauty of the key, and then many years later coming across a locked door which that very key (and no other) is able to open. Such a thing would never be expected, and so cries out for explanation.

Even though it is true that simple forms of mathematics were developed as methods to measure and quantify aspects of the physical world, the situation in physics is often quite different. Wigner said that "whereas it is unquestionably true that the concepts of elementary mathematics and particularly elementary geometry were formulated to describe entities which are directly suggested by the actual world, the same does not seem to be true of the more advanced concepts, in particular the concepts which play such an important role in physics."[13] The mathematical concepts pressed into service by physicists were previously devised by mathematicians who used them merely to demonstrate their own ingenuity and sense of formal beauty. Our laws of nature, which are formulated mathematically, are objects of complex applied mathematics. Alluding to the words of either Galileo or Kepler, Wigner remarked, "The statement that the laws of nature are written in the language of mathematics was properly made three hundred years ago; it is now more true than ever before."[14]

At one point in his essay, Wigner mentioned a related mystery: the fact that the human mind can carry out the convoluted mathematical reasoning required in the sciences; he said that "certainly it is hard to believe that our reasoning power was brought, by Darwin's process of natural selection, to the perfection which it seems to possess."[15] He went on to argue that "it is not at all natural that 'laws of nature' exist, much less that man is able to discover them."[16] He mused, "It is difficult to avoid the impression that a miracle confronts us here, quite comparable in its striking nature to the miracle that the human mind can string a thousand arguments together without getting itself into contradictions or to the two miracles of the existence of the laws of nature and of the human mind's capacity to divine them."[17] He offered no explanation for this miracle, and seemed resigned to the fact that it may ultimately be inexplicable:

> The miracle of the appropriateness of the language of mathematics for the formulation of the laws of physics is a wonderful gift which we neither understand nor deserve. We should be grateful for it and hope that it will remain valid in future research and that it will extend, for better or for worse, to our pleasure even though perhaps also to our bafflement, to wide branches of learning.[18]

Kepler: Mathematics and the Image of God

Johannes Kepler, one of the giants of the scientific revolution, believed that God created the cosmos according to a rational, mathematical plan and that, because we are able to investigate nature so effectively, the mind of man must have kinship with the mind of God. Even Kepler's self-written epitaph reflects his conviction that mind, with its mathematical aptitude, bears the image of the divine:

> Once I measured the skies,
> Now I measure the earth's shadow.
> Of heavenly birth was the measuring mind,
> In the shadow remains only the body.[19]

Two curious facts illustrate how striking the mathematics-nature correspondence is. First, as Wigner noted, there have been many cases in which a scientist has encountered a problem that required new mathematics only to discover that exactly the kind of tool he or she needed was already available. In other words, the mathematical system in question had been previously worked out by pure mathematicians—those who do math for math's sake regardless of any applicability it might have in the real world. The pre-existence of the right mathematics is a case of the scientist encountering a new lock only to find out that the pure mathematician constructed precisely the right key long ago. This is astounding! Contemporary atheist physicist Steven Weinberg has even admitted, "It is positively spooky how the physicist finds the mathematician has been there before him or her."[20]

Incidentally, *Donald in Mathmagic Land* gives an excellent example of the right mathematics long preceding its application in the sciences. In a brief animated sequence, the film shows how the planetary orbits can be modeled using the geometry of conic sections—the different "slices" that can be made through a cone that create specific kinds of curves such as the ellipse and the parabola. It was the ancient Greeks who first described the various curves of conic sections, but the geometry wasn't pressed into service to science until many centuries later, when Kepler used elliptical geometry to describe planetary motion and Galileo used parabolas in his analysis of terrestrial projectile motion. It's as if pure mathematics unconsciously anticipated the needs of future science and devised the perfect solutions. In *Mathematics and the Physical World*, mathematician Morris Kline argued that it is "unlikely that Kepler would have invented the ellipse to describe planetary motion, because that task, together with the one he actually performed of fitting the ellipse to the data, would have been superhuman."[21]

Another fine example Kline offered is how Albert Einstein was able to take full advantage of something called *Riemannian geometry* (developed more than a half century earlier) in his work on general relativity. Working out an ingenious new system of geometry and then applying it to a radically new theory of physics, said Kline, "would have been beyond the powers of one man."[22] The mathematical constructs were developed long in advance, without regard for their potential applicability to nature, and were ready and waiting when physics had progressed to the point of needing them. The situation is truly incredible, and it is difficult to believe that it is merely a case of happy cosmic coincidence.

The second curious fact that highlights the mystery of the deep interconnection between nature and mathematics is the fact that mathematics has enabled scientists to make successful predictions about physical reality. An impressive example of a fulfilled mathematical prediction was the confirmation of the existence of something called the *Higgs boson*, otherwise known as the *God particle*. Back in the 1960s, Peter Higgs and several other physicists were trying to determine how the subatomic particles that make up matter get their mass. By studying the behavior of the quarks that make up the protons and neutrons in the nuclei of atoms, these scientists were able to construct models of the fundamental structure of matter using mathematical equations based upon quantum physics. The problem was, if they tried to account for the particles' mass, what resulted was a messy and inconsistent heap of equations. But pretending that the particles had no mass at all produced splendidly elegant, symmetric mathematical patterns in their theory. It seemed like a catch-22.

Higgs came up with a possible solution; he proposed that fundamental particles get their mass from their environment—a field permeating all of space filled with some sort of undetected energy that exerts an opposing force on particles of matter when they accelerate. This resistance, argued Higgs, is interpreted by physicists as the particles' mass. This theoretical concept was dubbed the Higgs field, and gradually came to be accepted as a viable explanation; it allowed physicists to keep their aesthetically satisfying and consistent system of equations while still accounting for the mass of material entities. The important point here is that Higgs's *mathematical* theory predicted the existence of an unobserved *physical* entity—a pervasive field of energy through which everything moves.

Nearly four decades and one $10 billion international construction project later, physicists at CERN, the European Organization for Nuclear Research, were finally able to test for evidence of the theoretical

Higgs field. Near Geneva, Switzerland, crossing over the Swiss-French border and back, is a circular tunnel called the Large Hadron Collider (LHC). It is a high-tech underground racetrack of sorts that is more than sixteen miles in length and studded with thousands of super-conducting magnets that function to accelerate subatomic particles through the tunnel.

When particles collide with one another inside the LHC, special detectors record the explosive results, which constitute new data for physicists to incorporate into their theories. The calculations involved with the Higgs field theory indicated that collisions inside the LHC should cause reverberations in the field that cause it to occasionally fling off a mysterious signature particle—the Higgs boson. Such a particle would be so unstable that it would appear for only a tiny fraction of a second before it disintegrated back into the Higgs field, but it would leave behind evidence, a kind of fingerprint, that could be detected and then compared to the particle decay pattern predicted by the equations. Lo and behold, in early 2012, the data from the LHC confirmed Higgs's theory, fulfilling the prediction that came from the mathematical equations formulated decades before. "The Higgs field was predicted with a pencil," cosmologist Max Tegmark of MIT likes to quip.

What ramifications does this so-called "God particle" have for the question of the existence of a cosmic Creator? The popular media buzz at the time seemed to vaguely hint that the Higgs discovery had some sort of negative theological implications. This was simply a misconception based upon speculation about how the Higgs field could have been involved in sparking the big bang. (But even if it was, this still wouldn't eliminate an ultimate beginning of the cosmos and the need for a personal, immaterial cause.) When asked about the theistic or nontheistic implications of the Higgs field discovery, Dr. Peter Bussey, a particle physicist who works on the LHC, had this to say:

> It doesn't tell you anything about God, except that God is
> a mathematician, which is something we may like to talk

about. The fact that there's so much elegant mathematics underlying everything in the universe really does seem to suggest to me that there's a very clever intelligence there behind it all. If you look at the way the mathematics of the universe works, and how clever it is, you can't help feeling that to have this happen by accident is incomprehensible. There really needs to be some sort of Mind there, behind it all.[23]

Thus, instead of undermining the idea of a Creator, the Higgs field discovery re-emphasized the deep rationality of nature and mankind's ability to discern it, both of which beautifully support the Maker Thesis.

In light of the fact that mathematics has such direct applicability and predictive power in the natural sciences, it seems only reasonable to conclude that there is a real connection of some sort between the two, between abstract truths and the material world—which would mean nature is informed by Mind.

In his book *The Applicability of Mathematics as a Philosophical Problem*, Mark Steiner argues that the use of mathematics in sciences such as physics is inherently anthropocentric—human-centered. He explains that "relying on mathematics in guessing the laws of nature is relying on human standards of beauty and convenience," yet this approach has been used with great, undeniable success, playing a major role in the discoveries of physics.[24] This makes the universe appear to be remarkably "user friendly" for the human scientist, who has the intellectual capacity for mathematical analysis and a preference for elegant, "beautiful" mathematics rather than cumbersome and messy systems of equations.

> The fundamental structure of the world seems to be thoroughly rational, yet rationality is a characteristic of *mind*, and mind is necessarily *personal*.

Steiner considers this utility of mathematics to be a direct challenge to materialism; after all, why should abstract operations in the human mind have such descriptive and predictive power in the material realm if both are nothing more than matter behaving according to the laws of physics and chemistry? The fundamental structure of the world seems to be thoroughly rational, yet rationality is a characteristic of *mind*, and mind is necessarily *personal*. This strongly suggests that, in doing science, the mind of man is tapping into the work of a transcendent intelligence—the mind of the Maker, which doesn't sit well with those committed to materialism. The materialist needs a viable alternative explanation for the eerie applicability of mathematics to nature and the fact that mankind has the intellectual capacity necessary for the sophisticated mathematical reasoning needed in the sciences. To call these facts sheer happenstance seems to go well beyond the bounds of credulity.

Platonism to the Rescue?

Recall that the ancient Greek philosopher Plato believed that the physical world is patterned after immaterial, transcendent "Forms" that have real existence in an abstract realm, and that these Forms served as patterns for the creation of the tangible world. Max Tegmark of MIT is convinced that some version of Platonism—a real domain of abstract mathematical objects that is somehow "out there" and informing the material world—must be the reason for the rational structure of the universe. Tegmark's explanation is quite radical; he claims that the reason mathematics applies so well to the natural world and why we can discern and make sense of these patterns is that the cosmos (human minds included) is the material manifestation of a colossal mathematical entity. He says we are "self-aware parts of a giant mathematical object."[25] In his view, mathematics is the *essence of all reality*, much like the ancient Pythagoreans taught. According to Tegmark, we are parts of the physical actualization of an elaborate scheme that has only mathematical properties. He believes that this is precisely why the natural world exhibits rationality and why it is intellectually transparent to human beings.

Tegmark explains that if the cosmos is not fundamentally mathematical in a very real sense, then physics will one day hit an explanatory wall beyond which it cannot progress any further. In other words, once everything that can be described mathematically has been described, that will be the limit for the utility of physics, and all else will remain a permanent enigma. But if *everything* about the material world is indeed mathematical, then physics could one day reach that much-sought-after comprehensive and coherent "theory of everything."

The problem with Tegmark's theory is that it leaves us without an explanation for (1) the existence of an abstract realm of mathematical structures, and (2) how such immaterial entities manifest as physical phenomena. As Stephen Hawking asked, what breathes fire into the equations and produces the material world? In Tegmark's view, the ultimate explanation of the universe and our aptitude for its language is: because, mathematics. Yet this seems to leave an awful lot unanswered.

Roger Penrose's explanation for the applicability of mathematics to the natural world is a bit less bizarre than Tegmark's, but also has its fair share of loose ends. He rightfully admits that there is metaphysical (not scientific) mystery surrounding what he calls the "three worlds, three mysteries" problem. The "three worlds" he identifies are (1) the world of mathematics, (2) the mental world (human consciousness and rationality), and (3) the material world. (We've already seen that Penrose affirms a Platonic realm of mathematical truth, which he says is discovered, not invented.) The first mystery he identifies is the connection between the world of mathematics and the material universe, which is revealed, he says, by the fact that "operations of the physical world are now known to be in accord with elegant mathematical theory to an enormous precision."[26] "It makes no sense to me," he argues, "that this concurrence is merely the result of our trying to fit the observational facts into some organizational scheme that we can comprehend; the concurrence between Nature and sophisticated beautiful mathematics is something that is 'out there' and has been so since times far earlier than the dawn of humanity..."[27]

Thus, we have this material world that is for some reason mathematical, which leads to Penrose's second mystery: how the physical world and its processes gave rise to creatures with consciousness and rationality—the mental world that interacts with mathematics. Penrose asks:

> Is it merely the complication, or perhaps some other sophisticated quality, in the construction of our brains that allows for this mysterious phenomenon of consciousness to come about? And, if so, is this complication or sophistication to be understood in purely computational terms? If the latter, is this ingredient something lying hidden in the physics that we presently use for our descriptions of the operations of the world? Or must we search for deeper (mathematical?) theories for a physical description of consciousness to be possible? Or might we perhaps have to look even farther afield to an understanding that lies essentially beyond any kind of science whatever, as could be the implication of an essentially religious perspective on these issues?[28]

Is consciousness—which is a prerequisite for the rationality necessary for doing the mathematics of science—merely something that emerges from the material complexities of the brain that can themselves be described through mathematical physics, or is there something else going on that lies outside the scope of science?

Penrose speculates that our minds, because they are able to comprehend complex mathematical logic, may not be the product of physics alone, that "there must be something beyond our present-day physical laws that is operative in the actions of a conscious mind."[29] He says, "What really is going on in the activity of a conscious mind when it becomes convinced of the truth of some mathematical proposition remains profoundly mysterious."[30] It is not that science doesn't know but one day might; it is that the answer must be metaphysical because the questions themselves are philosophical, not scientific. Rather than entertaining the idea that there could be a nonmaterial facet to the human mind, Penrose deems the answer unknowable.

Penrose's third and final mystery is the fact that the mental world—the human mind—has access to the eternal, immaterial world of mathematics. If there is a Platonic domain existing beyond time, matter, and space, how is it that we (temporal, material beings) have come to know about it? If concepts like numbers and mathematical operations are just "out there," somehow informing the physical structure of all things, including the biological structures that must (if materialism is true) give rise to human consciousness and rationality, how is it that we have accessed these information-rich concepts, which are extrinsic to neurochemistry?

In an attempt to explain Penrose's three worlds, three mysteries, one could say, as Tegmark does, that mathematics is the fundamental reality that gives rise to everything else. But remember the problems associated with that view—the fact that it seems nonsensical to say that mathematics could *create* a material reality. Mathematical entities are not conscious agents with causal powers. Besides this, there's still the issue of how we could ever come to know about mathematical truths. Penrose's conclusion is that there is an ultimate reality that would bring coherence to the whole picture. We simply don't know, in his view, what that ultimate reality is—or could even possibly be.

Einstein's Miracle

Albert Einstein was captivated by the fact that our universe is structured in such a way that it corresponds with human rationality. He asked, "How can it be that mathematics, being after all a product of human thought independent of experience, is so admirably adapted to the objects of reality?"[31] In his famous essay entitled "Physics and Reality," he said about the universe: "The fact that it is comprehensible is a miracle."[32] Yet he was clear about his belief that science must remain content with having no way to explain this "eternal mystery of the world." "Oddly enough," he said, "we must be satisfied to acknowledge the 'miracle' without there being any legitimate way for us to approach it."[33]

Honesty About Materialism's Inadequacy

British physicist Paul Davies, who seems to ascribe to a pantheistic flavor of agnosticism, agrees that the mathematical structure of nature is discovered, not imposed upon nature by the human mind. Though most scientists take it for granted that natural laws are mathematical, the fact that mathematics applies "stunningly well" to the physical world, says Davies, "demands explanation, for it is not clear we have any absolute right to expect that the world should be well described by mathematics."[34] "Why," he asks, "should the mathematical approach prove so fruitful if it does not uncover some real property of nature?"[35] He refers to the secrets of the physical world as having been written in interconnected code that must be deciphered, much like a crossword puzzle. "What is remarkable," he says, "is that human beings are actually able to carry out this code-breaking operation, that the human mind has the necessary intellectual equipment for us to 'unlock the secrets of nature.'"[36] What makes this surprising is that the human mind is, allegedly, the product of unguided biological evolution, a process based upon survival and reproduction, not the higher cognitive abilities required to practice science. Davies says,

> One of the oddities of human intelligence is that its level of advancement seems like a case of overkill. While a modicum of intelligence does have a good survival value, it is far from clear how such qualities as the ability to do

advanced mathematics...ever evolved by natural selection. These higher intellectual functions are a world away from survival "in the jungle." Many of them were manifested explicitly only recently, long after man had become the dominant mammal and had secured a stable ecological niche.[37]

Davies recognizes that "there is no logical reason why nature should have a mathematical subtext in the first place, and even if it does, there is no obvious reason why humans should be capable of comprehending it."[38] Like Penrose, he speculates about some as-yet-to-be-discovered, or undiscoverable, principle inherent to nature that has allowed it to blindly engineer mental awareness and rationality: "Mindless, blundering atoms have conspired to make not just life, not just mind, but *understanding*. The evolving cosmos has spawned beings who are able not merely to watch the show, but to unravel the plot."[39] Davies considers currently available naturalistic explanations as well as theistic ones "either ridiculous or hopelessly inadequate."[40]

In his controversial book *Mind and Cosmos: Why the Neo-Darwinian Conception of Nature Is Almost Certainly False*, atheist philosopher Thomas Nagel argues that the fundamental cosmic reality cannot be explained by mindless physical processes. "The intelligibility of the world is no accident," he says. "Mind, in this view, is doubly related to the natural order. Nature is such as to give rise to conscious beings with minds; and it is such as to be comprehensible to such beings."[41] Human beings are the product "of the lengthy process of the universe gradually waking up and becoming aware of itself."[42]

Rather than espousing a theistic explanation for what we observe, Nagel (like Davies) is convinced that there is some unknown principle at work, a natural predisposition of the natural order to produce creatures with higher mental faculties that enable them to access things like mathematical truths. According to Nagel, the currently popular Darwinian approach will never be able to explain this principle of natural design, and thus needs to be revamped. He insists that we need "a much more radical departure from the familiar forms of naturalistic explanation"—if such a thing is even within the reach of human rationality.[43] In his earlier work, *The Last Word*, where he explored some of these same ideas, Nagel admits that his rejection of theistic explanations of the world are entirely philosophical: "I don't want there to be a God; I don't want the universe to be like that."[44] But interestingly, he concedes that his idea of a developmental principle in nature that has led to rational minds is compatible with the idea of divine creation.

Materialism is woefully inadequate for explaining the connections that exist between mathematics, the material world, and the human mind. As we have seen, even some eminent, nontheist contemporary scientists admit that this mystery is profound and seems to defy the explanatory power of the materialist paradigm. It seems absurd to dismiss this cosmic resonance as mere coincidence, yet if materialism is true, there is no other available option.

A More Satisfying Paradigm

The Maker Thesis has no difficulty explaining the objectivity of mathematical truth, how beautifully mathematics applies to physical reality, and mankind's corresponding intellectual capacities. If the cosmos is the creation of a rational Mind in whose image we are made, a Maker who desires our awareness of him, this deep interconnection makes perfect sense. As Oxford mathematician John Lennox has said, it is "not surprising when the mathematical theories spun by human minds created in the image of God's Mind find ready application in a universe whose architect was that same creative Mind."[45] Lennox echoes the theoretical physicist turned Anglican priest John Polkinghorne, who said, "The widespread success of science is too significant an issue to be treated as if it were a happy accident that we are free to enjoy without enquiring more deeply into why this is the case...I believe that a full understanding of this remarkable human capacity for scientific discovery ultimately requires the insight that our power in this respect is the gift of the universe's Creator who, in that ancient and powerful phrase, has made humanity in the image of God (Genesis 1:26-27)."[46]

For the materialist, the exquisite three-part harmony of mathematics, the human mind, and the material world is an enigma that the sciences will never have the tools to illuminate. However, if all things seen and unseen have the same rational source—the mind of the Maker—the mystery dissolves.

> For the materialist, the exquisite three-part harmony of mathematics, the human mind, and the material world is an enigma that the sciences will never have the tools to illuminate.

Key Points

- The universal, timeless nature of mathematical truths indicates that such truths are discovered rather than invented (though the language involved is indeed invented).

- Mathematics maps onto the natural world with an amazing precision that makes the natural sciences possible. The reason for this remarkable fit must be metaphysical rather than scientific.

- Repeatedly, scientists have identified a need for a new kind of mathematics for their theories only to discover that pure mathematicians had already developed just the right tools long before any application existed.

- Discoveries such as the Higgs field demonstrate the predictive power of the mathematics used in scientific theories.

- The higher rational faculties necessary for mathematical aptitude go far beyond the explanatory power of naturalistic evolutionary mechanisms.

- There is a strange resonance between mathematics, nature, and the mind of man; the Maker Thesis offers a satisfying explanation for this otherwise permanently inexplicable mystery.

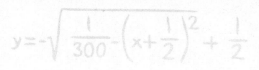

Chapter 10

Mind or Marionette?
Rationality and the Existence of the Soul

It is the spirit in man, the breath of the
Almighty, that makes him understand.

Job 32:8

"You," your joys and your sorrows, your memories and
your ambitions, your sense of identity and free will, are
in fact no more than the behavior of a vast assembly
of nerve cells and their associated molecules.[1]

Francis Crick

How can we square this self-conception of
ourselves as mindful, meaning-creating, free,
rational, etc., agents with a universe that consists
entirely of mindless, meaningless, unfree,
nonrational, brute physical particles?[2]

John Searle

I adore science fiction television and film. I'm delighted by intergalactic battles, parallel universes, and bizarre extraterrestrials. For me, another major appeal of sci-fi is how well the genre can spark important philosophical questions. Futuristic science and technology may lead one to ponder human nature—what we *are*—and related issues such as origins, consciousness, the afterlife, and the possibility of true artificial intelligence. As real-life technology advances, some sci-fi storylines strike us as more plausible than ever before. For instance, humanoid robots that are truly aware of the world and can think and feel in the same way human beings can don't seem that far-fetched in light of today's supercomputers. Sci-fi that speculates about such possibilities is great fun, but it raises profound questions that theists and materialists answer very differently.

The animated Disney/Pixar film *WALL-E* is a great example of sci-fi that communicates an interesting philosophical idea. Though the central character, WALL-E, looks nothing like a human being (he is, after all, a trash-compactor robot), he possesses attributes that we know, in reality, are exclusive to higher animals, including humans—things such as sentience and free agency. He is portrayed as a rational machine that experiences complex emotions and makes judgments about moral value and duty. This subtly suggests that sufficiently intricate circuitry is all that is needed to produce consciousness and the faculties we consider quintessentially human. If this is true, then it would not be unreasonable to believe that human beings are nothing more than highly sophisticated biological machines, and that there is no need to propose an immaterial component—what is typically referred to as a *soul*—to explain our distinguishing cognitive characteristics and abilities.

The question of the existence of the human soul, a debate that has been going on since antiquity, is relevant to the Maker Thesis in two ways. First, the historical, traditional Christian doctrine that humans are immaterial, immortal souls that are somehow integrated with a physical body is incompatible with the materialist understanding of the world.[3] Therefore, a strong argument for the soul undermines materialism while being favorable for theism. Second, there is a good case to be made for the claim that if the human soul did not exist, true rationality would be impossible. This chapter will first examine a few basic arguments for the existence of the soul before turning to the incompatibility of human rationality and materialism and the ramifications of the latter for the natural sciences.

Philosophy of mind, which is the branch of philosophy that deals with the question of the soul, is extraordinarily complicated; it involves specialized vocabulary, abstract concepts, and nuanced arguments that even some seasoned philosophers must work hard to properly engage with. That being said, what follows is a brief and simplified survey of a few arguments for the soul using everyday language where possible. Without a doubt, this introduction will lack many of the finer details involved in the academic discussion, but it should provide a general idea about the case for the soul and how it plays into the Maker Thesis.

What Is Man?

The materialist makes the philosophical assumptions that the world is a closed physical system and that there are no "outside," nonphysical entities that could interfere with its workings. Accordingly, he denies that there is an immaterial dimension of a human being that operates in conjunction with the body or survives its death. To be more precise with the vocabulary, *physicalism* is the idea that all that exists, including humans, are purely physical things. According to *reductive physicalism*, human beings are completely reducible to their physical properties. In this view, human beings can, in principle, be fully explained by the natural sciences; our first-person experience of the world and our mental activities are nothing more than neurochemical events. Consciousness, perceptions, desires, thoughts, agency, and higher reasoning are merely physical processes and are experienced by the brain rather than an immaterial self operating in conjunction with the brain. Basically, what we call the *mind* or the *mental* is simply brain chemistry.

Many physicalists, on the other hand, do not believe that the mental life can be entirely explained in physical terms and therefore hold a view called *nonreductive physicalism*, which says that there are mental states with mental properties that emerge from, but cannot be reduced to, physical properties. Thus, the nonreductive physicalist would affirm that states of consciousness—thoughts, beliefs, sensory experiences, and emotions—have mental properties that cannot be reduced to physical properties, but he would still insist that the *owner* of conscious states is the brain, not an immaterial soul or mind. Later on, the distinction between these two types of physicalism will be revisited, but for the time being, physicalism will be discussed in the general sense—the idea that human persons are entirely physical entities.

In contrast with physicalists, *substance dualists* believe that we humans are immaterial souls that work in conjunction with our bodies. In this view, the soul, not the brain, is what possesses mental properties such as consciousness and carries our personal identity—who we are, in essence. Put simply, human beings are made up of two substances: They have physical bodies with physical properties, and souls with mental properties. Some substance dualists would identify the mind with the soul, while other substance dualists would say that the mind is a faculty of the soul (I favor the latter view); either way, it is the soul which enables us to have sensations, thoughts, and beliefs as well as exercise free agency.

Substance dualists typically endorse something called *interactionism*, the idea that the brain and the soul have a two-way interactive relationship in which each can influence the other in certain ways. In other words, chemical events in the brain can cause what are referred to as mental events in the soul, but the reverse is also true; the soul itself is a free agent capable of causing desired brain events that can lead to things like purposefully moving the body, writing a poem, or working through an algebra problem.

A good (but admittedly imperfect) analogy for substance dualism-interactionism is the Marvel superhero Iron Man. Tony Stark is the intelligent agent—the "soul"—controlling the high-tech computerized robotic suit; but, as each film has shown, if damage occurs to the electronics or mechanics of the suit (the "body"), Stark is in trouble. Though he might be in first-rate shape, if his suit is not, his ability to function as Iron Man is inhibited. If the ocular cameras malfunction, he can't see; if the jets aren't working, he can't fly; if the robotics fail, he can't move about. If the suit shuts down entirely, Stark has to extricate himself to become unrestricted. Similarly, the soul's ability to exercise its capacities *while embodied* is dependent upon the fitness of the brain and body, which can be impaired by physical damage, disease, congenital disabilities, or certain kinds of drugs.

This is the gist of the two competing views being considered: Either we are immaterial souls operating symbiotically with our physical bodies (substance dualism), or we are physical beings and what we call the mental life is nothing more than our collective chemical brain states or properties that arise from them (physicalism). Contrary to what is often claimed, there are compelling philosophical and scientific reasons to believe that substance dualism is the correct understanding of human nature and that physicalism is false.

Leibniz's Law

Many people assume that neuroscientific studies are the only way to determine whether or not there is an immaterial soul that interacts with the material brain. However, making the case for or against substance dualism is largely (some would say entirely) a philosophical project rather than a scientific one. Let's consider a couple of philosophical arguments for the soul before turning to the topic of neuroscience.

Many contemporary substance dualists believe that something called *Leibniz's Law of the Indiscernibility of Identicals* (which I will call *Leibniz's Law* for short) can be used to argue that a soul—a *person*—is an entity that is distinct from the material brain. According to German philosopher Gottfried Wilhelm Leibniz (1646–1716), if X *is* Y, if they are one and the same thing, then everything that is true of X is also true of Y. If X has any property that Y lacks, or vice versa, then they are not what philosophers consider identical; they are not one and the same thing.

For instance, if my favorite flavor of ice cream (X) and Rocky Road ice cream (Y) are one and the same, then they have *all* and *only* the exact same properties (chocolate with nuts and marshmallows). It would be contradictory to say that my favorite flavor is identical to Rocky Road while also saying that my favorite flavor is pink and contains cherries, because if there is something true of my favorite flavor that is not true of Rocky Road, then they cannot be the same thing. Similarly, if a person is really only a brain in a body, then everything true of the brain is also true of the person, and vice versa. However, if we find that there is something true of one but not the other, then according to Leibniz's Law they cannot be the same thing—the person and his or her brain would be two distinct entities.

In his book *The Soul: How We Know It's Real and Why It Matters*, philosopher J.P. Moreland outlines two arguments for substance dualism that incorporate Leibniz's Law.[4] The first is based upon the indivisibility of human persons. We know from reflecting upon our own existence that we, as persons, are indivisible kinds of things—what Moreland refers to as "simple spiritual substances." As such, we cannot exist as fractions of ourselves. In other words, I know through introspection that I am a whole, indivisible person who is the owner of my experiences. If I lost a limb (or two or four), I would still be a complete *person* with an intact identity even if my body was not whole. The same is true for someone who has had part of his or her brain surgically removed due to a tumor or other disease. The patient would not be a percentage of a person as a result of the reduction in the mass of their brain tissue. Thus, physical bodies (and brains) are divisible, but persons are not—they are an all-or-nothing type of entity.

Moreover, a person has continuity of his existence, remaining the same thing over time (retaining his identity), whereas the body and brain follow a course of physical growth and development and come to have new parts over time through cellular regeneration. You are exactly the same person you were a year or decade ago (what Moreland calls an "enduring self"), even though the physical composition of your body and brain has changed. Therefore, under Leibniz's Law, physical bodies and persons are not identical; they must be distinct, separate things.

The second argument Moreland offers for substance dualism is based upon our first-person perspective of reality. Consider the fact that everything that is true of a physical object, such as a body or brain, can (at least in principle) be captured by a third-person description, while everything that is true of a person cannot. A neuroscientist could, theoretically, come to have comprehensive knowledge of your brain's anatomy and physiology, down to the behavior of every single molecule, but he could never have knowledge of your first-person experience of yourself. You are the only one who can know *what it is like*, from your own perspective, to be you. Moreland explains that

> no amount of third-person descriptions captures my own subjective, first-person acquaintance of my own self in acts of self-awareness...I know myself as a self immediately through being acquainted with my own self in an act of self-awareness. I can express that self-awareness by using the term *I*.
>
> *I* refers to my own substantial soul. It does not refer to any mental property or bundle of mental properties I am having, nor does it refer to any body described from a third-person perspective.[5]

Therefore, because of Leibniz's Law, a person, as a self, cannot be identical to their brain, because there is something true of the person that is not true of their brain.

Neuroscience and the Soul

Some physicalists contend that certain neuroscientific experiments indicate that mental experiences are identical to (the same thing as) brain events, and therefore offer empirical support for the physicalist position. What researchers have discovered is that various mental experiences can be induced by artificially stimulating specific parts of the brain, and the collective data have confirmed that activity in a particular region of the subject's brain consistently corresponds to a certain type of mental experience. For example, electrical stimulation of a precise location in the brain may reliably result in the subject's experience of a memory, a sensation such as a smell or taste, a feeling of sadness or euphoria, or an involuntary physical reaction.

Suppose you are the test subject in an experiment and, when the neuroscientist stimulates region A, you have the sensation of the smell of pineapple; when region B is stimulated, you have a mental image of your late grandmother's rose garden. Some physicalists believe that this correlation between a brain state and a mental experience demonstrates that one's mental life is really nothing but the sum of one's brain states. However, this argument has a major flaw: It does not actually prove that brain states and mental states are one and the same thing (recall Leibniz's Law). Moreland argues that "just because A *causes* B (or vice versa), or just because A and B are *constantly correlated* with one other, that does not mean that A is identical to B."[6] Neuroscience is indeed able to show that there is a *correlation* between the mind and brain activity, or that brain events can *cause* mental events, but it is not able to show that the two are one and the same thing, and therefore it cannot rule out the existence of the soul as the seat of mental events.

Are States of Consciousness Merely Physical Brain States?

States of consciousness include things like thoughts, beliefs, and sensations. There is a good reason to believe that these are not merely states of the material brain: Unlike brain states, conscious states are not accessible by a third-person observer. Suppose a neuroscientist is monitoring your brain activity while you, unbeknownst to her, have an orange for a snack. As you bite into a piece of the orange, taste receptors on your tongue transmit chemical signals through a network of nerves to the region of your brain associated with taste. The neuroscientist may be able to determine that you're having a taste sensation, but she cannot know anything of your personal experience—what the taste is like *to you*. If she sliced open your brain, she would fare no better; the subjective taste sensation of the orange cannot be found somewhere in your grey matter. The scientist would have to ask you what kind of sensory experience you're having, and the best you could do is verbally describe it as a sweet, tangy, orange-y taste, but that still wouldn't give her first-person knowledge of what your sensation is like. Similarly, she would not be able to access your thoughts and beliefs through empirical investigation. We should therefore conclude that conscious states are not identical to physical brain states.

The substance dualist fully recognizes that brain events can be the cause of mental experiences. A nonartificial example would be instances of bodily injury; the damaged part stimulates nerves to fire in a pathway leading to the brain, causing an event in the brain that produces the conscious experience of being in pain. However, this doesn't mean that the neurons firing in the brain *are* the first-person pain sensation. Another example would be visual perception; light waves bounce off an object such as an apple, hit the receptors on the retina of the eye, which send signals along the optic nerve to the brain. Brain activity then produces the subjective visual sensation of the apple. However, the substance dualist would add that causation in the other direction (mind to brain) can also be the case; in other words, just as brain activity can be the cause of a mental experience, immaterial mental activity can be the cause of a physical reaction in the brain.

For instance, when we intentionally recall the details of a past event, execute a purposeful behavior, or carry out complex mental processes such as mathematics, the mind's intentional activity is impacting the brain—the mind is somehow bringing about the associated brain activity required to achieve its purpose. A good example would be playing a musical instrument. When I sit down at a piano, it is my brain activity that causes my fingers to move across the keys, but it is my mind which produces the intentions that inform my brain in terms of when and how to move each of my fingers.

Even though neuroscience can neither confirm nor rule out the existence of the soul, there is interesting neuroscientific evidence from which it is reasonable to infer that the mind is (or is a faculty of) an agent who can freely manipulate his or her own brain activity. Dr. Jeffrey Schwartz is a research psychiatrist at UCLA's School of Medicine and one of the world's leading experts in neuroplasticity—the brain's ability to reorganize and make new connections between neurons in response to a new physiological situation. From his intensive and lengthy studies involving patients with obsessive-compulsive disorder (OCD), Dr. Schwartz has discovered that the purposeful actions of the mind can cause changes in the neurochemical pathways in the brain—that neuroplasticity can be self-directed through intentional mental exercises.

Rather than using pharmaceuticals to treat his patients, Dr. Schwartz has trained them to use mindful, meditative techniques to gain control over their obsessive-compulsive thoughts and behaviors. When OCD patients have followed this regimen over a period of time, they have been able to transform their own brain chemistry, reroute neural pathways, and recover from their debilitating disorder to an impressive degree. Their *minds* have successfully impacted their *brains* in an observable way. It seems fair to say that Dr. Schwartz's research has provided scientific evidence that the mind has some causal power over the brain, that it is not simply the impotent by-product of brain activity.

Dr. Schwartz's methods have even been used in the entertainment industry. In an effort to get into character for the film *The Aviator*, which is about the life of severe OCD sufferer Howard Hughes, Leonardo DiCaprio consulted with Dr. Schwartz to learn the thought patterns and behaviors of real OCD patients. Later, it was reported that it took DiCaprio more than a year of using Dr. Schwartz's therapeutic techniques to reverse the changes that had occurred in his brain as a result of deliberately thinking and acting in an obsessive-compulsive manner throughout the making of the film.[7] This seems like good evidence that the conscious mind can work to manipulate the brain, thereby causing physical reactions and long-term change. There is genuine agency involved, which, as we will discuss momentarily, requires a freedom that a fully material entity cannot have, since such an entity operates entirely based upon undirected physical cause and effect.

> The mind—the self—is an agent that transcends the brain yet can exert some control over its function.

The key point that Dr. Schwartz's research seems to demonstrate is that the mind can *freely choose* to act in a certain way: It can voluntarily follow specified instructions in an effort to override biology-based psychological tendencies, achieve a desired change in brain activity, and, eventually, rewire neural pathways. This indicates that the mind—the self—is an agent that transcends the brain yet can exert some control over its function.

Free Mental Agency and Rationality

Physicalism carries an enormous consequence: If it is true, then free agency is an illusion. What we perceive as intentional physical and mental activities are entirely the result of material processes in the brain over which we have no actual control. As Moreland notes, "If physicalism is true, then human free will does not exist...If I am just a physical system, there is nothing in me that has the capacity to freely choose to do something."[8] If the soul does not exist, there seem to be only two possible physical explanations for the brain states that lead to the mental and physical actions we perceive as voluntary:

1. Each brain state is caused by the one preceding it, and
   that one was caused by the one before it, and so on and so
   forth, like billiard balls colliding. You can think of it as one
   long, inevitable chain reaction of neurochemical events
   (often influenced by environmental input) that could be
   fully predicted if one had comprehensive knowledge of

the movement of every particle that makes up the physical world.

2. Brain states are caused by blind neurochemical processes, but at the subatomic level, there is an element of randomness (so-called quantum indeterminacy) that makes it impossible to predict, with 100 percent accuracy, exactly what is going to happen in the brain from one moment to the next.

In both cases, the brain states that give rise to mental or physical actions are physical, produced by blind molecules acting according to natural law, and there is no such thing as authentic free agency. As atheist neuroscientist Sam Harris says:

> Free will is an illusion. Our wills are simply not of our own making. Thoughts and intentions emerge from background causes of which we are unaware over which we exert no conscious control. We do not have the freedom we think we have...Either our wills are determined by prior causes and we are not responsible for them, or they are the product of chance and we are not responsible for them.[9]

For Harris, the factors at play in our mental activity are things like our genetic makeup—which determines much of our brain anatomy and physiology—and the impact of our environment on our brain chemistry. For instance, we could say that a genetic predisposition combined with the psychological stress of a horrific childhood caused a particular man to commit homicide later in life. If physicalism is true, the man did not freely make a rational decision to kill, and he couldn't have chosen to do otherwise. He may have acted in accordance with a desire, but his desire was determined by material factors, and he was powerless to resist it. The front cover of Harris's book features a picture of marionette puppet strings, which is clever and quite fitting given his view. If there is no free will, then we are indeed nothing more than meat puppets performing in blind obedience to the puppet masters: our DNA and physical environment.

Pascal: Thinking Souls, Not Thinking Matter

Blaise Pascal was a seventeenth-century French mathematician, physicist (to use the modern term), and Catholic theologian. He was a proponent of substance dualism, and although his scholarly legacy does not include a major work on human nature, his view is revealed in a posthumous compilation of his fragmentary notes known as the *Pensées*. In Section II, Pascal said,

> [W]e are composed of two opposite natures, different in kind, soul and body. For it is impossible that our rational part should be other than spiritual; and if any one maintain that we are simply corporeal, this would far more exclude us from the knowledge of things, there being nothing so inconceivable as to say that matter knows itself. It is impossible to imagine how it should know itself. So, if we are simply material, we can know nothing at all. [10]

Pascal draws a direct connection between the immateriality of the soul (our "spiritual" part) and human rationality, and considers the notion of thinking material stuff to be an absurdity. After all, how is it that matter could have conscious experiences and contemplate abstract ideas? This theme is also apparent in Pascal's pithy remark, "Philosophers who have mastered their passions. What matter could do that?" [11] In other words, if our physical makeup naturally produces instincts and desires that we can, through conscious effort, control, there must be an immaterial entity freely exerting control over the brain.

If there is no true free agency, the activities that we normally consider to be under our control really are not. For example, suppose you've been inspired by a wonderful work of literature and you set out to write the great American novel. As you sit at your computer, pouring out the words of the story, setting the scenes and developing your characters, you may think *you* are in control of the creative process to a significant extent, that you *freely* craft the plotline, invent the characters, and choose the linguistic style in which to write the story. However, if physicalism is true, then the novel you produce is nothing more than the inevitable result of physics and chemistry. As atheist philosopher Thomas Nagel explains, "There is no room for agency in a world of neural impulses, chemical reactions, and bone and muscle movements."[12]

Common sense about our personal everyday experience tells us that we are in fact agents who often freely choose things like how we move our bodies, what words we speak, and what we focus our thoughts upon. The substance dualist argues that our common sense about personal free agency is correct, that our souls are agents interacting with our physical brain to bring about our desired behaviors and mental activities.

Yet if physicalism is true, our intuition about being free agents is illusory; we are nothing more than biological machines whose mental activity is (one way or another) the result of neurochemistry. What we perceive as our conscious choices are actually produced by inevitable physical processes in the brain over which we have no directive control. If this is right, then the entire edifice of human civilization is the result of blind matter in motion and nothing more; once science has gained comprehensive knowledge of the material world, everything—rationality, creativity, love, hate, etc.—will be fully explained in physical terms. As atheist philosopher Richard Rorty put it, "Every speech, thought, theory, poem, composition, and philosophy will turn out to be completely predictable in purely naturalistic terms. Some atoms-and-the-void account of micro-processes within individual human beings will permit the prediction of every sound or inscription which will ever be uttered. There are no ghosts."[13] (By "ghosts," Rorty meant immaterial souls.)

Recall from early in the chapter that nonreductive physicalists include nonphysical mental *properties* in their account of the human person. Typically, this is a move to retain physicalism while preserving things like our commonsense understanding of mental causation—our ability to intentionally cause our own mental activity and physical behavior. Nonreductive physicalism says that free agency is a function of the mental states that arise from our brains. However, even some philosophers who reject the existence of a soul have persuasively argued that nonreductive physicalism does not succeed in preserving genuine free agency.[14] If there are mental states that somehow emerge from the material brain states, as the nonreductive physicalist claims, those brain states are still dependent upon prior physical states and are therefore inevitable, not freely chosen by an agent. Moreland explains that, in order to have real free agency, what is needed is an immaterial "I"—a self who can intervene in the physical workings of the brain according to a conscious intention.[15] Unfortunately for the nonreductive physicalist, there is no convincing account for how the alleged emergent mental states could exert causal power over the material brain; such states do not rescue free agency.

Setting aside the serious issue of moral responsibility, there is another devastating consequence if there is indeed no free agency: Genuine rationality would be impossible. Consider the following. When presented with a set of observations that we analyze in an effort to reach an explanatory conclusion, we must be able to make free choices during the process of mental deliberation, taking into account all sorts of information along the way and reconciling that information with what we already know to be true in order to reach a sensible conclusion. This step-by-step practice includes making unfettered judgments about the observations in question and drawing appropriate connections to known facts using the rules of good reasoning. However, if all our brain activity is beyond our conscious control, then the necessary free agency for such deliberation doesn't exist.

We have no good reason to believe that blind material processes—molecules inevitably behaving according to the
laws of nature—are in any sense truth-aimed.

It is interesting to note that some great scientists and mathematicians of previous centuries realized that there is a serious problem
for rationality, as commonly understood, if our mental activity is
entirely physically determined. Sir Arthur Eddington, a central figure
of twentieth-century physics, penned an essay entitled "The Decline of
Determinism," in which he emphasized the relationship between free
agency and trustworthy human reason:

> Suppose I have hit on a piece of mathematical research
> which promises interesting results. The assurance that I
> most desire is that the result which I write down at the
> end shall be the work of a Mind which respects truth
> and logic, not the work of a hand which respects [laws
> of nature such as] Maxwell's equations and the conserva-
> tion of energy...But the truth of the result of 7 x 11 = 77
> lies in its character as a possible mental operation and not
> in the fact that it is turned out automatically by a special
> combination of cog-wheels...If the mathematical argu-
> ment in my mind is compelled to reach the conclusion
> which a deterministic system of physical law has preor-
> dained that my hands shall write down, then reasoning
> must be explained away as a process quite other than that
> which I feel it to be. But my whole respect for reasoning
> is based on the hypothesis that it is what I feel it to be.[16]

In other words, if human thought is nothing more than inevitable
material processes instead of a free deliberation that intentionally
applies the abstract rules of sound reasoning to immaterial conceptual content in the mind, then true rationality does not exist. Implicit
in Eddington's statement is the point that rationality requires a Mind

that can consciously direct its own activity to arrive upon truth (such as mathematical solutions) through correct reasoning. However, we have no good reason to believe that blind material processes—molecules behaving according to the laws of nature—are in any sense truth-aimed.

Thomas Reid: Only Free Minds Write Poetry and Do Science

Thomas Reid, the eighteenth-century Scotsman who became known as the Common Sense philosopher, was clearly a proponent of substance dualism. In describing human persons he said, "By the *mind* of a man, we understand that in him which thinks, remembers, reasons, wills...We define *body* to be *that which is extended, solid, movable, divisible*. In like manner, we define *mind* to be *that which thinks*...and this principle of thought we call the *mind* or *soul* of man."[17]

Notice how Reid emphasized that the body, not the mind, is divisible and that it is the mind, not the body, which thinks, reasons, and wills. Reid explained that material bodies behave according to the forces acting *upon* them, whereas the mind is, by nature, an agent that can act *freely*. He understood that true rational activity can exist only if the mind has the power to self-direct its train of thought. In other words, if we do not control our own thinking, then true rationality, as we commonly define it, doesn't exist.

Moreover, if we are not agents with the power to direct our mental actions, how is it that products of our mind can purposefully conform to external standards? Reid argued, "No man can believe that Homer's ideas...arranged themselves according to the most perfect rules of epic poetry; and Newton's according to the rules of mathematical composition."[18] Based upon the fact that mental output can follow nonphysical standards, such as the guidelines of epic poetry and mathematics (to use Reid's examples), we should conclude that the outcome of reasoning is not merely the result of a chain of blind physical processes that, by definition, can have no conscious objective.

J.B.S. Haldane (1892–1964), an atheist who was highly educated in both mathematics and the biological sciences, held a similar view about the ramifications of the materialist view of human persons. He said, "If materialism is true, it seems to me we cannot know that it is true. If my opinions are the result of the chemical processes going on in my brain, they are determined by chemistry, not the laws of logic."[19] In other words, blind chemical processes cannot take principles of good reasoning into account and therefore do not constitute genuine rationality (even though such processes could *accidentally* produce a result that conforms to the laws of logic). Later, Haldane changed his mind due to the development of early computers—machines that could function according to the rules of mathematics—and embraced a fully materialist view of the human mind. However, one could argue that Haldane made a mistake in thinking that brains are like computers, since computers are able to operate in a specific way only because an intelligent agent programmed them with the capacity to do so. Computers could easily be designed to use faulty logic because there is nothing about their nature that is concerned with truth. For that, free agency is required.

Einstein's Predicament

Einstein believed that the world is a closed system that operates according to deterministic material processes. He insisted that nothing can miraculously intervene in the physical order from the "outside," the way the God of monotheism is purported to do. Einstein included human beings in his deterministic view, thereby denying that we have authentic free will. Because of this,

he rejected the notion of divine reward and punishment, since neither could be truly deserved if a person's behavior is governed by
the laws of nature. (Yet, paradoxically, Einstein was highly critical
of the actions of the Nazis.) But if Einstein was right about everything in the world being physically determined, that means his own
brain chemicals simply reacted in just the right way to produce
the theory of general relativity and there is no personal agent who
deserves credit for that brilliant achievement.

Hermann Weyl (1885–1955), a German theoretical physicist and
mathematician who contributed to cosmology and quantum mechanics, also saw the insurmountable problem the materialist understanding of human nature posed for rationality. In his book *Mind and
Nature*, he said, "When I reason that 2 + 2 = 4, this actual judgment
is not forced upon me through blind natural causality (a view which
would eliminate thinking as an act for which one can be held answer-
able) but something purely spiritual enters in: the circumstance that 2
+ 2 really equals 4, exercises a determining power over my judgment."[20]
Weyl seems to mean that when we reason, we are able to take truth into
account and freely direct our mental processes toward it. If the mind is
wholly the result of inevitable physical processes, it simply turns input
into output by way of neurochemical reactions that can have no concern for truth.

A similar line of thinking has carried over into contemporary substance dualism. Moreland explains that if brain activity is determined
by physics and chemistry, then "there is only one outcome possible,
and it was fixed prior to the act of deliberation by forces outside the
agent's control."[21] He notes that when we work through a mental chain
of reasoning in search of the truth, we not only weigh the relevant evidence, we assign different levels of importance to each piece of evidence being considered; this requires free agency, which cannot exist
if physicalism is true. It seems that there is authentic rationality only if

there is an agent that transcends the brain and can freely direct mental processes according to the informational content involved and the abstract principles of sound reasoning. The most viable (perhaps only) explanation for this transcendent agent is an immaterial soul that is not entirely restricted by physical cause and effect, a free mind somehow acting through the physical brain. Philosopher Angus Menuge has argued that "[i]f we want to account for consciousness, mental causation and reasoning, we need some entity over and above the body. This entity must be simple, have thoughts as inseparable parts, persist as a unity over time, and have active power. That sounds like a soul."[22]

Rationality and the Natural Sciences

Contemporary philosopher Roger Trigg points out that a physicalist conception of human rationality cannot explain the sciences. He says, "Science assumes as a basis for its own existence the presence of a human rationality that rises above the linkages between cause and effect. The production of science cannot itself be part of a normal causal process... The practice of science depends on weighing arguments to see how strong the evidence is and even to decide what is to count as evidence or what is irrelevant to the matter in hand. Science cannot avoid the recurrent issue of truth."[23] He goes on to say that if everything, including the brain, is entirely the result of law-governed material processes, "No room is left for the exercise of reason. The kind of reality envisaged by physicalism cannot allow for the independent reality of mind, belief, or reason. All is in physical form and physically determined."[24]

The problem this poses for the scientist who holds to physicalism is inescapable. He must come to grips with the fact that science depends upon the assumption that true rationality exists, yet that assumption cannot be supported by the physicalist worldview. Think back to chapter 9, which discusses the mathematical structure of nature and the necessity of mathematics in scientific activities. If rational deliberation is needed anywhere, to be sure it is needed in mathematical calculations and their correct application to scientific investigation. Recall that mathematical truths exist objectively and eternally, outside of space and time. Moreland has pointed out that if our minds are only physical, there can be no explanation for how they have come to know such things, because "to know mathematical truths, [one] must have a soul or mind that has the innate power to grasp non-physical, abstract objects."[25] Otherwise, how would a physical brain come to have knowledge of something that cannot impact it on a physical level?

> Science depends upon the assumption that true rationality exists, yet that assumption cannot be supported by the physicalist worldview.

Without the ability to reason mathematically—which requires free agency—most (if not all) advancements in the natural sciences would have been impossible. If physicalism is true, we are not free agents, and therefore, we aren't in control of the outcome of our mental processes. Therefore, it seems reasonable to say that, at the least, the observable success of the natural sciences is good evidence for the existence of a free agent—the soul. In this way, the sciences themselves are excellent support for the Maker Thesis.

Key Points

- Physicalism is the view that humans are merely the sum of their material parts.

- Nonreductive physicalists recognize that consciousness (and its states, such as sensations, beliefs, and thoughts) is not reducible to physical description, but nevertheless maintain that consciousness is only a product of physical brain activity.

- Substance dualism-interactionism says that human persons are immaterial souls integrated with physical bodies and that the soul and brain interact in a two-way relationship. The mind is (or is a faculty of) the soul rather than a by-product of neurochemical activity.

- Leibniz's Law of the Indiscernibility of Identicals can be used in arguments for substance dualism because brains and persons have different properties.

- Neuroscientific experiments do not eliminate the possibility of the soul. Constant correlation of brain states with mental experiences or a causal relationship between the two doesn't prove that the two are one and the same.

- Therapy developed for OCD patients, in which voluntary repetitive mental exercises have been shown to rewire the brain over time, strongly suggests that a human being is made up of an agent that has the power to manipulate some brain activities.

- If physicalism is true, all mental activity is determined by a chain of underlying blind causes. In that case, there is no such thing as genuine free agency.

- Free agency is required for rationality, such as logical and mathematical deliberation. Therefore, a free agent, which cannot be wholly material, is essential to the natural sciences.

- The amazing success of the natural sciences serves as compelling evidence for the existence of the soul.

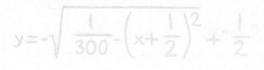

Chapter 11

The Maker Thesis: Putting the Pieces Together

Like a musician who has tuned his lyre, and by the artistic blending of low and high and medium tones produces a single melody, so the Wisdom of God, holding the universe like a lyre, adapting things heavenly to things earthly, and earthly things to heavenly, harmonizes them all, and leading them by His will, makes one world and one world order in beauty and harmony.[1]

St. Athanasius

God created the human race, not in a vacuum, but as part of a created order in which he manifests himself. And in the created order, the divine *Logos* is a principle of unity and purpose, and rationality.[2]

Michael Ramsey

In his famous work of apologetics entitled *Orthodoxy*, G.K. Chesterton said that he was convinced of the truth of Christianity not because of any one specific piece of evidence, but because of "an enormous accumulation of small but unanimous facts."[3] He compared the fit between Christian teachings and our observations of the world to a superbly tailored coat that, when tried on, "fits in every crease."[4] Furthermore, Chesterton said, when you have *diverse* evidence for a truth claim rather than lots of similar evidence from only one or two areas, the overall case is even more compelling: "The very fact that the things are of different kinds increases the importance of the fact that they all point to one conclusion."[5]

To better appreciate what Chesterton means about the power of diverse evidence, imagine a crime scene—a burglary, perhaps—in which a single fingerprint lifted from the scene is found to match someone's print in the police database. This fingerprint would be a good reason to classify that person as a suspect, but perhaps not enough for a prosecutor to get a conviction.

Now suppose this suspect's fingerprints were found in dozens of places throughout the scene. This would comprise better evidence. But what if, in addition to fingerprints, detectives were able to gather incriminating DNA samples, security camera footage, and an eyewitness description of a car registered to the suspect? This final scenario would provide a much more powerful implication of the suspect's guilt.

In this spirit, the preceding chapters have presented support for the Maker Thesis using a variety of evidence from several different disciplines. Rather than just one or two bits of curious data, we have an accumulation of assorted facts from cosmology, physics, earth science, neuroscience, philosophy of mind, and biochemistry that all seem to be leading to the same conclusion: the existence of a Maker of all things who made us in his image and gave us a cosmic home in which the natural sciences can thrive.

The overarching goal of this book has been to reveal the harmonious, unifying framework that the Maker Thesis provides for scientific evidence gleaned from observable reality in conjunction with philosophical argumentation. Recall the peg-puzzle analogy introduced in chapter 1; the Maker Thesis represents the puzzle board with a background image and uniquely shaped cutouts, and the evidence from the different scientific and philosophical disciplines represents the pieces. When these pieces are set into place, the completed picture beautifully explains the intriguing hints we previously noticed around the edges of the pieces, how they seem to point beyond themselves to a higher reality. We see that they are all related to one another within a unifying context. In this way, the Maker Thesis makes sense of the world we live in; it provides a perfect fit for different phenomena that otherwise (under materialism) must be seen as nothing more than a series of incredibly fortunate accidents that happened to occur at just the right time, in just the right place. Ultimately, the Maker Thesis is far more intellectually satisfying than the alternative of materialism.

> The Maker Thesis makes sense of the world we live in; it provides a perfect fit for different phenomena that otherwise (under materialism) must be seen as nothing more than a series of incredibly fortunate accidents that happened to occur at just the right time, in just the right place.

A Survey of the Pieces

Let's briefly revisit each puzzle piece.

Piece #1: A Finite Universe

In chapter 3, we examined the scientific evidence and the philosophical arguments for a finite universe—an ultimate beginning of matter and space-time itself. In the twentieth century, astronomers discovered that space is expanding at a high rate of speed, continually increasing the distance between galaxies and galaxy clusters. Their observational data was confirmation of the prediction made by Einstein's theory of general relativity (and Friedmann and Lemaître's mathematical solutions). More recently, the Borde-Guth-Vilenkin theorem (or BGV theorem) demonstrated that any feasible cosmological model requires an ultimate beginning. This is the idea behind the big bang theory, which postulates the sudden emergence of the universe—all matter, energy, and space-time itself—from a cosmic singularity, prior to which there was *nothing at all.*

The scientific evidence for a finite universe serves as excellent support for a philosophical argument for God's existence known as the *kalam* cosmological argument. According to this argument, everything that begins to exist has a cause for its beginning, and because the universe began to exist, it must have had a cause. Any candidate for this cause must transcend the universe itself and have powers of causation, which means that it is a timeless, immaterial agent. This is, at a very basic level, what Christianity understands God to be.

Some have responded that there must have been a state of affairs prior to the big bang (such as a quantum vacuum field) that would explain why the universe came into being. Besides the fact that there is no scientific support for this hypothesis, it runs headlong into a major philosophical problem: the impossibility of an infinite series of past moments or events. In other words, if there was a material cause of the big bang, what caused that cause and the cause before that, and so on? To say that the causes go back eternally (an infinite regress) doesn't work, for it is impossible to travel through an infinite series of past events to get to the moment of the big bang.

A Maker who brought all things into being from nothing is by far the best explanation for the beginning of the universe; this idea makes sense of the science and avoids the insurmountable philosophical problems that plague materialist theories.

Piece #2: A Universe Fine-Tuned for Life

In the second part of chapter 3, we explored the overwhelming evidence for cosmic fine-tuning, the uncontroversial idea that many physical parameters of the universe (constants and quantities) are aligned with an enormous degree of precision that permits the existence of any kind of life. For example, the gravitational constant is fine-tuned to one part in 10^{60}, and the density of so-called dark energy is fine-tuned to one part in 10^{120}. The list of physical constraints that must fall within an extraordinarily narrow range has only grown longer as cosmologists learn more about the deep structure of the universe. It is highly improbable that a mindless process would produce the level of fine-tuning necessary for a life-permitting universe.

In an attempt to explain away the fine-tuning problem, some materialists have suggested that our universe is only one part of a massive multiverse—an ensemble of worlds that each have randomly ordered physical constants and quantities. The idea is that our universe is just one of the very few lucky ones that just happen to be life-permitting; with so many universes popping into existence throughout eternity, eventually there would be one like ours, with the constants and quantities necessary for complex life. Unfortunately for multiverse theorists, there is no observational evidence for the necessary kind of multiverse; moreover, the theory cannot avoid the philosophical problems associated with past infinities. Multiverse theories are essentially philosophical speculation meant to circumvent the fine-tuning problem.

A "theory of everything" that would explain why all the constants and quantities of the universe *must* be what they are would not solve the fine-tuning problem. It wouldn't answer the question of why we have a life-permitting state of affairs instead of a *far* more probable lifeless universe. However, the intentional creation of a world that permits life—intelligent life, no less—is well explained by the Maker Thesis.

Piece #3: A World Just Right for Complex Life and Scientific Discovery

Chapter 5 showcased several examples of another amazing "coincidence"—the fact that some features of the universe and our planetary home that are hospitable to complex life-forms—such as human beings—are the very same features that facilitate scientific discovery. For example, controllable fire that burns hot enough to smelt metals is made possible by the right kind of atmosphere, which happens to be the kind of atmosphere necessary for any kind of respiration in larger animals. Moreover, the fuels and raw materials needed for metallurgy are present on earth in abundance, and human beings have the intelligence and dexterity to harness fire and manufacture metals. Otherwise, significant scientific progress would have been impossible.

Another fascinating example of habitability coinciding with discoverability is the phenomenon of perfect solar eclipses. Such eclipses provide a wealth of information to astronomers, such as the chemical composition of the sun and distant stars. A range of factors must come together to make perfect eclipses possible, such as Earth's distance from the sun and the size, shape, and orbital distance of a planet's moon. These factors are also important to the earth's habitability; our moon is large enough, but not too large, to stabilize Earth's rotation axis at a degree of tilt that moderates the global climate. In addition, our planet's distance from the sun allows for plentiful liquid water that isn't all locked up in glaciers, as well as a regular rotation that produces cycles of day and night (another climate-moderating mechanism). Moreover, the light spectrum that makes perfect eclipses so informative is the range of light wavelengths needed for high-definition vision as well as any type of plant photosynthesis. That's a remarkable threefold coincidence all on its own.

It didn't have to be the case that the features and conditions that make complex life possible are also those that facilitate scientific advancement. We could have existed in a world that permitted the flourishing of higher life-forms but not the activities that led to many indispensable scientific discoveries and resulting technologies. The fact that so many characteristics of Earth and our solar system coincide to allow both intelligent life and science to flourish clearly points to the existence of a Mind who desired the success of the sciences.

Piece #4: The Biochemical Design of Life

In chapter 6, we took a historical detour to examine eighteenth- and nineteenth-century design arguments that were held in high esteem in the years following the scientific revolution, including William Paley's watchmaker argument. We saw that although Charles Darwin sought to give an account for the diversity and complexity of life that excluded divine agency, some of his contemporaries who supported the theory of evolution by natural selection still believed that the design of living things pointed to a Maker. The point being, Darwin did not demolish design arguments forevermore; those who argue to the contrary are adding materialist philosophy onto evolutionary theory. Whether or not the theory is correct is a separate question.

Chapter 7 discussed the rise of modern molecular biology that was triggered by Watson and Crick's discovery of the DNA double helix followed by the confirmation of Crick's hypothesis about the sequence of DNA bases determining the code for the construction of proteins. DNA exhibits the characteristic of sequence specificity, which means that the arrangement of its parts determines its message. When that message is translated into amino acid chains, the sequence specificity of the amino acids determines the folding of the completed protein molecule and thus the function the protein can carry out in the cell.

Materialist origin-of-life scenarios that seek to account for the first self-replicating molecules fall short of demonstrating that there is a feasible path from dead chemicals to the first information-bearing molecules capable of reproducing and undergoing natural selection. For one thing, the conditions on the early Earth would not have been conducive to the chemical reactions needed to produce the necessary building blocks. For another, scientists attempting to construct the self-replicating ribozymes that would have populated the theoretical RNA world have inadvertently shown that brilliant minds and lots of intervention are required to make progress toward forming a self-replicating molecule from scratch. Essentially, this supports the argument for the intelligent design of life. Even if a pathway is found that could have occurred on its own on the early Earth, the problem does not truly go away, for we now know how many finely tuned conditions are necessary to even get the right starter molecules, let alone an entire living cell.

The "junk" DNA argument for naturalistic evolution has been debunked, and researchers continue to find functions for DNA sequences once thought to be evolutionary leftovers. The usefulness of far more of the genome than previously recognized arguably points to intentional design rather than an unguided trial-and-error process.

As a storage medium, DNA is unsurpassed. Scientists have been able to encode complex manmade data onto strands of DNA and later translate the biochemical code back into the original information. This demonstrates that DNA is not simply *like* a high-tech storage medium; it actually *is* one. Biochemist Fazale Rana contends, in what he calls a "reverse Watchmaker" argument, that this kind of biomimicry is excellent evidence of design. In addition to DNA, there are many other examples of systems in nature being copied by human engineers to create or improve human technologies.

The Maker Thesis superbly explains the sophisticated design of DNA and solves the problems faced by naturalistic theories of the origin of life. Moreover, it makes sense of the fact that, as with the mathematical physical sciences, human beings have the intellectual capability to delve into the complexities of life at its molecular level—a fact that defies the materialist paradigm.

Piece #5: A Mathematically Structured, Comprehensible Cosmos

As chapter 9 explained, the sciences owe their existence to the fact that our universe is fundamentally mathematical. Many eminent thinkers have argued that mathematical truths are discovered, not invented; they are the kinds of truths that are objective and eternal, whether mankind is here to know them or not. Quite mysteriously, mathematics maps onto the physical world with a precise hand-in-glove fit, and this correspondence is vital to many scientific fields, such as physics and cosmology. The field of pure mathematics—mathematics for its own sake rather than for any possible applicability to physical reality—has yielded systems that later became useful to a new scientific problem, much like a pre-existing key fitting a brand new lock.

> According to Christian theism, God reveals his wisdom and power to mankind through the creation, and it is fitting that this natural revelation would eventually involve science and mathematics—two of our more awe-inspiring intellectual achievements.

Mathematics has also made predictions about physical reality that later turned out to be true, as in the case of the Higgs field. To top it all off, there is a congruence between the mathematically comprehensible universe and the intellectual aptitude of mankind. There is no good reason to expect that the higher cognitive capabilities required for sophisticated mathematics would emerge as a result of naturalistic evolutionary processes. This three-way resonance of mathematics, mind, and matter cries out for explanation. Nontheists such as Roger Penrose, Max Tegmark, and Thomas Nagel, who realize that this situation cannot simply be dismissed as a cosmic accident, have suggested that mathematics or mind somehow underlies all of reality. Yet this does not ultimately explain the existence of mathematical truths, how such abstract entities would inform the material world, and how modern evolutionary theory could account for beings with the advanced intellect required for higher mathematical reasoning.

If there is a Maker of all things, including human beings bearing his image, it is not surprising that the physical world has a rational structure that is congruent with the mind of man. According to Christian theism, God reveals his wisdom and power to mankind through the creation, and it is fitting that this natural revelation would eventually involve science and mathematics—two of our more awe-inspiring intellectual achievements.

Piece #6: Human Nature and Scientific Rationality

Chapter 10 examined the question of the existence of the human soul. The traditional Christian view (substance dualism) is that human beings are immaterial souls integrated with a physical body. This stands opposed to the physicalist view, which says that human beings are nothing more than the sum of their physical parts and biological processes. Several good philosophical arguments that incorporate Leibniz's Law can be used to show that persons are not their physical bodies or brains. The two have different properties, which means they cannot, logically speaking, be one and the same.

Neuroscientific data cannot rule out the existence of the soul. The most it can do is demonstrate that there are consistent correlations between some mental experiences and certain brain states or that some brain states stand in causal relationship to particular mental experiences. These facts do not show that the mind simply *is* the brain. Research involving OCD patients and neuroplasticity has indicated that persons are free agents who can manipulate their own brain activity, leading to physiological changes. This supports the idea that there is a mind or soul that transcends the material brain yet can interact with it in a causal manner—which is entirely consistent with substance dualism but not with physicalism.

The physicalist pays a high price: If physicalism is true and humans are wholly material creatures, then all mental activities are determined by blind physical events, which means that free agency in thought and behavior is an illusion. (Some philosophers of mind dispute this claim, but even some nontheist philosophers have convincingly argued that free agency is incompatible with physicalism.) If there is no free agency in our mental life, there can be no authentic rationality. Without true rationality, which is required to carry out things like mathematical deliberation, the sciences could not exist. The fact that the natural sciences have been so successful is powerful evidence for free mental agency—which, in turn, supports the case for the soul.

Science and the Mind of the Maker

The Maker Thesis is a unifying and logical framework for all six of these pieces. It offers a satisfying explanation for the origin, rationality, and intricacy of nature as well as the stunning fact that the natural world is comprehensible to the human mind. If there is a Maker behind the cosmos in whose image we are made, then the astounding success of the sciences is no mystery; the Christian theist should expect that his or her mind has a special kinship with a Mind who desires to be known through his creation. By illuminating nature through scientific study, mankind demonstrates the kind of being he is and gains a wondrous glimpse into the mind of the Maker.

Materialism utterly fails to provide a sufficient explanation for any of the aforementioned pieces, and it cannot even begin to explain why all of them harmonize in a way that makes the natural sciences possible. To say that blind natural processes are responsible for this multifaceted cosmic "coincidence" goes far beyond the bounds of credulity. The materialist is left with many unanswerable questions, dead-end brute facts, and physical features of the universe that just happen to exist at the right place at the right time. This is a disjointed and unsatisfying view of reality from both an intellectual and spiritual perspective. Concerning the latter, Alister McGrath has said, "We long for some reassurance of the *coherence of reality*—that however fragmented our world of experience may seem, there is a half-glimpsed 'bigger picture' which holds things together, its threads connecting together in a web of meaning that might otherwise seem incoherent and pointless."[6] Materialism does not deliver.

In an essay entitled "Is Theology Poetry?" C.S. Lewis wrote:

> Christian theology can fit in science, art, morality, and the sub-Christian religions. The scientific point of view cannot fit in any of these things, not even science itself. I believe in Christianity as I believe that the Sun has risen, not only because I see it, but because by it I see everything else.[7]

Lewis's point is that Christianity brings an unparalleled lucidity to the human experience of the world; Christianity makes sense of things, whereas materialism (what he refers to as the "scientific point of view") cannot even provide an adequate justification for science itself. Lewis's sun analogy is perfect; Christian theism, which includes the Maker Thesis, brilliantly illumines every aspect of cosmic reality, while materialism leaves a great deal in permanent shadow.

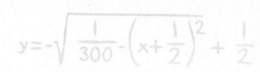

Notes

Prologue: Science as the Experience of a Masterpiece

1. Peter Kreeft, *Socratic Logic* (South Bend, IN: St. Augustine's Press, 2010), 144.

2. Richard Swinburne, *Is There a God?* (New York: Oxford University Press, 1996), 68.

3. Dorothy Sayers, *The Mind of the Maker* (San Francisco: HarperCollins, 1987), 49.

Chapter 1—The Science and Faith Conversation: Understanding the Lay of the Land

1. Steven Weinberg, *Facing Up* (Cambridge: Harvard University Press, 2001), 242.

2. G.K. Chesterton, *The Club of Queer Trades* (New York: Harper & Brothers, 1905), 241.

3. Jerry Coyne, *Faith vs. Fact* (New York: Penguin Books, 2016 edition), xii.

4. Coyne, *Faith vs. Fact,* xii.

5. Coyne, *Faith vs. Fact,* 29.

6. Coyne, *Faith vs. Fact,* 133.

7. Neil deGrasse Tyson, in *Cosmos: A Spacetime Odyssey.*

8. Stephen Hawking and Leonard Mlodinow, *The Grand Design* (New York: Bantam Books, 2010), 5.

9. Roger Trigg, *Beyond Matter* (Conshohocken, PA: Templeton Press, 2015), 21.

10. Richard Lewontin, "Billions and Billions of Demons," *New York Review of Books,* January 9, 1997.

11. Alister McGrath, *Christian Theology: An Introduction* (West Sussex: John Wiley & Sons, 2017), 142.

12. Quoted in Alister McGrath, *Re-Imagining Nature* (West Sussex: John Wiley, 2017), 174.

Chapter 2—The Divine in Nature: A Big (and Ancient) Idea

1. Vergil, *The Aeneid* (New Haven: Yale University Press, 2008), 138.

2. Cicero, *The Nature of the Gods* (New York: Oxford University Press, 2008), 48.

3. Cicero, *The Nature of the Gods,* 13.

4. Plato, *Timaeus* (Indianapolis: Focus, 2016), 14.

5. Plato, *Timaeus,* Great Books of the Western World, vol. 6, 2d ed. (Chicago: Encyclopaedia Britannica, Inc., 1990), 455.

6. Plato, *The Republic,* 396.

7. Plato, *The Republic.*

8. John Dillon, *The Middle Platonists: 80 BC to AD 220* (Ithaca, NY: Cornell University Press, 1996), 139.

9. Philo, "On the Creation," in *The Works of Philo*, trans. C.D. Yonge (Peabody, MA: Hendrickson Publishers, 1993), 4.

10. Philo, "On the Creation," 5.

11. Dillon, *The Middle Platonists*, 95.

12. See William Lane Craig's treatment of this topic in "God and the Platonic Host," in *C.S. Lewis at Poet's Corner* (Eugene, OR: Wipf & Stock, 2016), 204.

13. *Wisdom of Solomon*, accessed January 23, 2017 at http://www.catholic.org/bible/book .php?id=27&bible_chapter=13.

14. *Wisdom of Solomon*.

15. Nicomachus, Great Books of the Western World, vol. 10, 2d ed. (Chicago: Encyclopaedia Britannica, Inc., 1990), 596.

16. Nicomachus, *Introduction to Arithmetic*, Book I, Great Books of the Western World, vol. 10, 2d ed. (Chicago: Encyclopaedia Britannica, Inc., 1990), 601.

17. Nicomachus, *Introduction to Arithmetic*, 601-602.

18. Socrates Scholasticus, *Historia Ecclesiastica* IV, 23.

19. Clarence Glacken, *Traces on the Rhodian Shore: Nature and Culture in Western Thought from Ancient Times to the End of the Eighteenth Century* (Berkeley, CA: University of California Press, 1976), 203.

20. Athanasius, *Against the Heathen* 44.3 and 45:1-2. In *Nicene and Post-Nicene Fathers of the Christian Church*, vol. IV, eds. Philip Schaff and Henry Wace (Peabody, MA: Christian Literature Company, 1892), 23.

21. Alister McGrath, *Christian Theology* (West Sussex: Blackwell Publishing Ltd., 2017), 145.

22. Augustine, *Sermons: 51-94* (Hyde Park, NY: New City Press, 1991), 225-226.

23. Henry Wadsworth Longfellow, excerpt from *The Fiftieth Birthday of Agassiz*, May 28, 1857.

24. Augustine, *Eighty-three Different Questions* in *The Fathers of the Church*, vol. 70 (Washington, DC: CUA Press, 2010), 81.

25. Augustine, *On Genesis* (New York: New City Press, 2002), 246.

26. Augustine, *On Genesis*, 248.

27. Augustine, *Eighty-three Different Questions*, 81.

28. See David Lindberg, *The Beginnings of Western Science* (Chicago: University of Chicago Press, 2007), 156.

29. Giuseppe Tanzella-Nitti, "The Two Books Prior to the Scientific Revolution," *Perspectives on Science and Christian Faith* 57, no. 3 (September 2005): 238.

30. Tanzella-Nitti, "The Two Books."

31. Lindberg, *The Beginnings of Western Science*, 209.

32. John of Salisbury, *The Metalogicon* (Philadelphia: Paul Dry Books, 2009), 29.

33. John of Salisbury, *The Metalogicon*, 133.

34. John of Salisbury, *The Metalogicon*, 227.

35. Tanzella-Nitti, "The Two Books," 241.

36. Tanzella-Nitti, "The Two Books."

37. Tanzella-Nitti, "The Two Books," 242.

Chapter 3—The Origin and Structure of the Cosmos: Finite and Finely Tuned

1. Robert Jastrow, *God and the Astronomers* (New York: Warner Books, 1980), 3-4.

2. Arno Penzias, quoted in William Dembski, *Signs of Intelligence* (Grand Rapids: Brazos Press, 2001), 168.

3. John Farrell, *The Day Without Yesterday* (New York: Thunder's Mouth Press, 2005), 100.

4. Fred Hoyle, *The Intelligent Universe* (New York: Holt, Rinehart, and Winston, 1983), 13.

5. Stephen M. Barr, *The Believing Scientist* (Grand Rapids: Eerdmans Publishing, 2016), 128.

6. Television interview accessed on YouTube, July 19, 2017, https://youtu.be/jDSvYLtYdxo.

7. Jastrow, *God and the Astronomers*, 5.

8. "A Scientist Caught Between Two Faiths: Interview with Robert Jastrow," *Christianity Today*, August 6, 1982.

9. Arvind Borde, Alan H. Guth, and Alexander Vilenkin, "Inflationary spacetimes are not past-complete," *Physical Review Letters*, 90, 151301 (April 15, 2003).

10. Alexander Vilenkin, "The Beginning of the Universe," *Inference: International Review of Science*, vol. 1, issue 4 (October 23, 2015).

11. Vilenkin, "The Beginning of the Universe."

12. Aristotle, *On the Heavens*, Book II, Section I.

13. William Lane Craig, *On Guard* (Colorado Springs: David C. Cook, 2010), 74.

14. Craig, *On Guard*, 84.

15. Craig, *On Guard*, 75.

16. See the outstanding books by cold-case homicide detective and Christian case-maker J. Warner Wallace.

17. Craig, *On Guard*, 108.

18. Stephen Hawking, *The Grand Design* (New York: Bantam, 2010), 161-162.

19. Freeman Dyson, *Disturbing the Universe* (New York: Harper & Row, 1979), 250.

20. Fred Hoyle, quoted in Owen Gingerich, "The Universe as Theatre for God's Action," *Theology Today*, vol. 55 (October 1998), 311.

21. Robin Collins, "The Teleological Argument: An Exploration of the Fine-Tuning of the Universe," in *The Blackwell Companion to Natural Theology*, eds. William Lane Craig and J.P. Moreland (West Sussex: John Wiley & Sons Ltd., 2012), 215.

22. Geraint Lewis and Luke Barnes, *A Fortunate Universe* (Cambridge: Cambridge University Press, 2016), 158.

23. Lewis and Barnes, *A Fortunate Universe*, 159.

24. Hugh Ross, *The Creator and the Cosmos* (Colorado Springs: NavPress, 2001), 149.

25. For an extensive list, see Hugh Ross, *The Creator and the Cosmos* (Colorado Springs: NavPress, 2001).

26. Lewis and Barnes, *A Fortunate Universe*, 13.

27. George F.R. Ellis, "Does the Multiverse Really Exist?" *Scientific American*, August 2011.

28. George Ellis interview on whyarewehere.tv.

Chapter 4—Priests in God's Cosmic Temple: Natural Revelation and the Scientific Revolution

1. John Milton, *Paradise Lost*, in *Book of the Cosmos,* ed. Dennis Danielson (Cambridge, MA: Perseus Books, 2001), 204.

2. Tommaso Campanella, *Apologia Pro Galileo*, in *Book of the Cosmos*, 176.

3. Rodney Stark, *For the Glory of God* (Princeton: Princeton University Press, 2003), 138.

4. Copernicus, *Revolutions of the Heavenly Spheres*, reprinted in *The Book of the Cosmos*, 106-107.

5. Letter to J.G. Herwart von Hohenburg, 16 February 1605, *Johannes Kepler Gesammelte Werke*, ed. M Caspar et al., Munich, 1937, vol. 15, 146.

6. Carola Baumgardt, *Johannes Kepler: Life and Letters* (New York: Philosophical Library, 1951), 33-34.

7. Baumgardt, *Johannes Kepler*, 50.

8. Baumgardt, *Johannes Kepler*.

9. Gerald Holton, *Thematic Origins of Scientific Thought* (Cambridge: Harvard University Press, 1988), 68.

10. Johannes Kepler, *Conversation with Galileo's Sidereal Messenger* (New York: Johnson Reprint Corp., 1965), 43.

11. Baumgardt, *Johannes Kepler*, 41.

12. Johannes Kepler, *Harmonies of the World*, trans. Charles Glenn Wallis (Annapolis, MD: St. John's Bookstore, 1939), Kindle Loc. 259.

13. Alistar McGrath, *Re-Imagining Nature*, (West Sussex: John Wiley, 2017), 82.

14. Quoted in Morris Kline, *Mathematics: The Loss of Certainty* (New York: Oxford University Press, 1980), 31.

15. Quoted in Morris Kline, *Mathematics: The Loss of Certainty* (New York: Oxford University Press, 1980), 31.

16. Baumgardt, *Johannes Kepler*, 44.

17. Maurice Finocchiaro, *The Essential Galileo* (Indianapolis: Hackett Publishing, 2008), 110.

18. Finocchiaro, *The Essential Galileo*, 119.

19. Finocchiaro, *The Essential Galileo*, 183.

20. Finocchiaro, *The Essential Galileo*, 116.

21. Galileo, *Dialogue Concerning the Two Chief World Systems*, trans. Stillman Drake (Berkeley, CA: University of California, 1962), 11-12.

22. Joseph Spence and John Underhill, *Spence's Anecdotes, Observations, and Characters of Books and Men* (London: W. Scott, 1890), 70.

23. A conviction plainly expressed in the second edition of his *Opticks* (1717).

24. Isaac Newton, General Scholium to the *Principia Mathematica*, 3d ed., 1726.

25. A.R. Hall and M.B. Hall, *Unpublished Scientific Papers of Isaac Newton* (Cambridge: Cambridge University Press, 1962), 141.

26. Snezana Lawrence and Mark McCartney, eds., *Mathematicians and Their Gods* (Oxford: Oxford University Press, 2015), 124.

27. A.R. Hall and M.B. Hall, *Unpublished Scientific Papers of Isaac Newton*, 141.

28. Angus Menuge, ed., *Reading God's World* (St. Louis, MO: Concordia Publishing House, 2004), 71.

29. Menuge, ed., *Reading God's World*, 71.

30. Gary Ferngren, *Science & Religion* (Baltimore, MD: Johns Hopkins University Press, 2002), 165.

31. J.J. MacIntosh, *Boyle on Atheism* (Toronto: University of Toronto Press, 2005), 241. Spellings in this citation and the following are faithful to the original.

32. MacIntosh,, *Boyle on Atheism*, 233.

33. MacIntosh, *Boyle on Atheism*, 239.

34. MacIntosh, *Boyle on Atheism*, 234.

35. MacIntosh, *Boyle on Atheism*, 384.

Chapter 5—Habitable and Discoverable: A World Just Right for Scientists

1. *Der Spiegel*, issue 42 (October 17, 1988). Accessed at http://www.spiegel.de/spiegel/print/d-13542088.html.

2. Guillermo Gonzalez and Jay Richards, *The Privileged Planet* (Washington, DC: Regnery Publishing, 2004), xv.

3. Gonzalez and Richards, *The Privileged Planet*, 60.

4. Darwin, *Descent of Man* (New York: American Home Library Company, 1902), 73.

5. Robin Collins, Plantinga Conference at Baylor University, November 7, 2014.

6. Benjamin Wiker and Jonathan Witt, *A Meaningful World* (Downers Grove, IL: InterVarsity Press, 2006), 164.

7. Michael Denton, *Fire-Maker* (Seattle: Discovery Institute Press, 2016), 24.

8. Denton, *Fire-Maker*, 27.

9. Denton, *Fire-Maker*, 23.

10. Wiker and Witt, *A Meaningful World*, 167.

11. Gonzalez and Richards, *The Privileged Planet*, 66.

12. Michael Denton, *Nature's Destiny* (New York: Free Press, 1998), 62.

13. Denton, *Nature's Destiny*, 62.

14. George Greenstein, *The Symbiotic Universe* (New York: William Morrow, 1988), 96-97.

15. Gonzalez and Richards, *The Privileged Planet*, 67.

16. Gonzalez and Richards, *The Privileged Planet*.

17. Denton, *Nature's Destiny*, 53.

18. Gonzalez and Richards, *The Privileged Planet*, 66.

19. Sir Isaac Newton, *Opticks* (1704), Book 1, Part 2, Exper. XV, 114.

20. Gonzalez and Richards, *The Privileged Planet*, 17.

21. Gonzalez and Richards, *The Privileged Planet*, 9.

22. Gonzalez and Richards, *The Privileged Planet*, 4-5.

23. Gonzalez and Richards, *The Privileged Planet*, 6-7.

24. Gonzalez and Richards, *The Privileged Planet*, 18.

25. Hugh Ross, *Improbable Planet* (Grand Rapids: Baker Books, 2016), 44.

26. Gonzalez and Richards, *The Privileged Planet*, 115.

27. Ross, *Improbable Planet*, 46.

28. Carl Sagan, *Pale Blue Dot* (New York: Random House, 1994), 26.

Chapter 6—A Death Knell for Design Arguments? Natural Theology and Darwin's Response

1. Charles Darwin, *On the Origin of Species* (Cambridge: Harvard University Press, 2003), 488.

2. William Paley, *Natural Theology* (New York: Oxford University Press, 2008), 9.

3. Ernst Mayr, *The Growth of Biological Thought* (Cambridge: Belknap Press, 2003), 515.

4. Paley, *Natural Theology*, 7.

5. Paley, *Natural Theology*, 8.

6. Cicero, *The Nature of the Gods* (New York: Oxford University Press, 2008), 78.

7. James Hannam, *The Genesis of Science* (Washington, DC: Regnery Publishing, 2011), 158-159.

8. Paley, *Natural Theology*, 16.

9. Paley, *Natural Theology*, 199.

10. Paley, *Natural Theology*, 200.

11. Paley, *Natural Theology*.

12. Paley, *Natural Theology*, 254.

13. Paley, *Natural Theology*, 218.

14. Paley, *Natural Theology*, 219-220.

15. Paley, *Natural Theology*, 222.

16. Nora Barlow, ed., *The Autobiography of Charles Darwin 1809–1882* (London: W.W. Norton & Company, 1958), 57.

17. Barlow, *The Autobiography of Charles Darwin*, 57.

18. Barlow, *The Autobiography of Charles Darwin*, 58.

19. Barlow, *The Autobiography of Charles Darwin*, 59.

20. Darwin, *On the Origin of Species*, 130.

21. Darwin, *On the Origin of Species*, 484.

22. Barlow, *The Autobiography of Charles Darwin*, 92-93.

23. Barlow, *The Autobiography of Charles Darwin*, 93.

24. Barlow, *The Autobiography of Charles Darwin*, 94.

25. Alfred Russel Wallace, *The World of Life* (London: Chapman and Hall, 1914), vi-vii.

26. Charles Darwin, *The Correspondence of Charles Darwin, Volume 8, 1860* (Cambridge: Cambridge University Press, 1993), 303.

27. Asa Gray, *Darwiniana; Essays and Reviews Pertaining to Darwinism* (Amazon Digital Services, 2012), Kindle Loc. 829.

28. Gray, *Darwiniana*, Kindle Loc. 969.

29. Gray, *Darwiniana*, Kindle Loc.

30. Gray, *Darwiniana*, Kindle Loc. 652.

31. Gray, *Darwiniana*, Kindle Loc. 763.

32. Gray, *Darwiniana*, Kindle Loc. 1609.

33. Thomas H. Huxley, "Criticisms on 'The Origin of Species'" in *Collected Essays by T.H. Huxley*, vol. 2 (New York: Greenwood Press, 1968), 82.

34. John Hedley Brooke, "Myth 25: That Modern Science Has Secularized Western Culture," in *Galileo Goes to Jail and Other Myths About Science and Religion*, ed. Ronald Numbers (Cambridge: Harvard University Press, 2009), 227.

35. Jon H. Roberts, "Myth 18: That Darwin Destroyed Natural Theology," in *Galileo Goes to Jail and Other Myths About Science and Religion*, ed. Ronald Numbers (Cambridge: Harvard University Press, 2009), 163.

Chapter 7—The Language of Life: The Marvels of DNA

1. Quoted in Roger Highfield, "Do our genes reveal the hand of God?" *The Telegraph* (London), March 20, 2003.

2. Quoted in "God Is Not Threatened by Our Scientific Adventures," www.beliefnet.com.

3. A 90 percent complete draft was published in February 2001.

4. J.R.R. Tolkien, *The Lord of the Rings* (New York: Houghton Mifflin, 1991), 32.

5. Charles Darwin, *On the Origin of Species* (Cambridge: Harvard University Press, 2003), 484.

6. Darwin Correspondence Project at University of Cambridge, LETT 7471.

7. Stephen C. Meyer, *Signature in the Cell* (New York: HarperCollins, 2009), 301.

8. Fazale Rana, *Creating Life in the Lab* (Grand Rapids: Baker Books, 2011), 171.

9. Rana, *Creating Life in the Lab*.

10. Rana, *Creating Life in the Lab*.

11. Rana, *Creating Life in the Lab*, 180.

12. Richard Dawkins, *The Greatest Show on Earth* (New York: Free Press, 2009), 333.

13. Kenneth R. Miller, "Life's Grand Design," *Technology Review* 97 (February-March 1994).

14. Richard Dawkins, *A Devil's Chaplain* (New York: Mariner Books, 2004), 99.

15. Dawkins, *The Greatest Show on Earth*, 332.

16. Francis Collins, *The Language of God* (New York: Free Press, 2006), 136.

17. The ENCODE Project Consortium, "An Integrated Encyclopedia of DNA Elements in the Human Genome," *Nature* 489 (September 6, 2012), 57-74.

18. Jonathan Wells, *The Myth of Junk DNA* (Seattle, WA: Discovery Institute Press, 2011), 50.

19. Fazale Rana, *The Cell's Design* (Grand Rapids: Baker Books, 2008), 259.

20. Rana, *The Cell's Design*.

21. Robert Service, "DNA could store all of the world's data in one room," *Science* (March 2, 2017).

22. Richard Dawkins, *River Out of Eden* (New York: Basic Books, 1995), 18-19.

23. Bill Gates, *The Road Ahead* (New York: Penguin Books, 1996), 228.

24. Yaniv Erlich and Dina Zielinski, "DNA Fountain enables a robust and efficient storage architecture," *Science*, vol. 355, issue 6328 (March 2017): 950-954.

25. Fazale Rana, "Insect Biology Advancing Technology" in *God & the World of Insects*, ed. Josh Shoemaker and Gary Braness (Silverton, OR: Lampion Press, 2017).

26. Rana, "Insect Biology Advancing Technology."

27. Rana, "Insect Biology Advancing Technology."

Chapter 8—Revival of the God Hypothesis: Twentieth-Century Physics and Cosmology

1. G.K. Chesterton, *The Everlasting Man* (Seaside, OR: Rough Draft Printing, 2013), 7.

2. E=hf, where the energy (E) is calculated by multiplying the frequency (f) of the radiation by a number now known as *Planck's constant* (h).

3. Max Planck, *Scientific Autobiography*, in Great Books of the Western World, vol. 56 (Chicago: Encyclopaedia Britannica, Inc., 1990), 110.

4. Planck, *Scientific Autobiography*, 116.

5. Planck, *Scientific Autobiography*.

6. Planck, *Scientific Autobiography*.

7. Planck, *Scientific Autobiography*, 117.

8. Brian Greene, *The Elegant Universe* (New York: W.W. Norton & Company, 2003), 50.

9. Max Jammer, *Einstein and Religion* (Princeton, NJ: Princeton University Press, 1999), 48.

10. Jammer, *Einstein and Religion*.

11. Jammer, *Einstein and Religion*, 93.

12. Albert Einstein, *The World as I See It* (New York: Kensington, 2006), 31.

13. Albert Einstein, *Letters to Maurice Solovine* (Paris: Gauthier-Vilars, 1956), 102-103.

14. Albert Einstein, in a letter to Maurice Solovine dated March 30, 1952. Accessed February 2, 2017 at http://inters.org/Einstein-Letter-Solovine.

15. Albert Einstein, "Physics and Reality" (1936).

16. See Matthew Stanley's excellent discussion of this in his introduction to *Practical Mystic: Religion, Science, and A.S. Eddington* (Chicago: University of Chicago Press, 2007).

17. Arthur Eddington, *The Expanding Universe* (New York: Cambridge University Press, 1988), 55.

18. Eddington, *The Expanding Universe*.

19. Eddington, *The Expanding Universe*, 56.

20. Eddington, *The Expanding Universe*, 60.

21. Eddington, *The Expanding Universe*, 125.

22. Eddington, *The Expanding Universe*.

23. Eddington, *The Expanding Universe*, 94.

24. Eddington, *The Expanding Universe*, 95.

25. Eddington, *The Expanding Universe*, 95-96.

26. Arthur Eddington, *Science and the Unseen World* (New York: MacMillan Company, 1929), 27-28.

27. Eddington, *Science and the Unseen World,* 28-29.

28. Eddington, *Science and the Unseen World,* 57.

29. Eddington, *Science and the Unseen World,* 65.

30. Eddington, *Science and the Unseen World,* 67.

Chapter 9—A Meeting of the Minds: Our Comprehensible Mathematical Universe

1. St. Augustine, *City of God,* 11.30.

2. Maurice Finocchiaro, *The Essential Galileo* (Indianapolis: Hackett Publishing, 2008), 183.

3. Bertrand Russell, *Principles of Mathematics,* vol. I (London: Cambridge University Press, 1903), 451.

4. G.H. Hardy, *A Mathematician's Apology* (Cambridge: Cambridge University Press, 2012), 123-124.

5. Along with Stephen Hawking, Penrose demonstrated the necessity of a cosmic singularity at the beginning of space-time (the Hawking-Penrose theorem) and thereby earned the 1988 Wolf Prize in physics.

6. Roger Penrose, "Is Mathematics Invented or Discovered?" Interview on PBS's *Closer to Truth.*

7. Roger Penrose, "Is Mathematics Invented or Discovered?"

8. Max Tegmark, *Our Mathematical Universe* (New York: Vintage Books, 2015), 260.

9. Eugene Wigner, "The Unreasonable Effectiveness of Mathematics in the Natural Sciences," reprinted in *The World Treasury of Physics, Astronomy, and Mathematics,* ed. Timothy Ferris (Boston: Little, Brown & Co., 1991), 527.

10. Wigner, Eugene, and Andrew Szanton, *The Recollections of Eugene P. Wigner* (Cambridge, MA: Basic Books, 2003), 39.

11. Wigner and Szanton, *The Recollections of Eugene P. Wigner,* 60.

12. Wigner, "The Unreasonable Effectiveness of Mathematics in the Natural Sciences," 527.

13. Wigner, "The Unreasonable Effectiveness of Mathematics in the Natural Sciences," 528.

14. Wigner, "The Unreasonable Effectiveness of Mathematics in the Natural Sciences," 532.

15. Wigner, "The Unreasonable Effectiveness of Mathematics in the Natural Sciences," 528.

16. Wigner, "The Unreasonable Effectiveness of Mathematics in the Natural Sciences," 531.

17. Wigner, "The Unreasonable Effectiveness of Mathematics in the Natural Sciences," 533.

18. Wigner, "The Unreasonable Effectiveness of Mathematics in the Natural Sciences," 540.

19. James Voelkel, *Johannes Kepler and the New Astronomy* (New York: Oxford University Press, 1999), 130.

20. Steven Weinberg, "Lecture on the Applicability of Mathematics," *Notices of the American Mathematical Society* 33.5 (October), quoted in Mark Steiner, *The Applicability of Mathematics as a Philosophical Problem* (Cambridge: Harvard University Press, 1998).

21. Morris Kline, *Mathematics and the Physical World* (New York: Dover Publications, 1959), 473.

22. Kline, *Mathematics and the Physical World,* 473.

23. Peter Bussey, video interview in *God and the Big Bang: how the universe began—the moment of creation*, produced by www.focus.org.uk.

24. Mark Steiner, *The Applicability of Mathematics as a Philosophical Problem* (Cambridge, MA: Harvard University Press, 1998), 7.

25. Max Tegmark, *Our Mathematical Universe* (New York: Vintage Books, 2015), 271.

26. Roger Penrose, "Mathematics, the mind, and the physical world," in John Polkinghorne, ed., *Meaning in Mathematics* (New York: Oxford University Press, 2011), 44.

27. Roger Penrose, "Mathematics, the mind, and the physical world," 44-45.

28. Roger Penrose, "Mathematics, the mind, and the physical world," 42-43.

29. Roger Penrose, "Mathematics, the mind, and the physical world," 43.

30. Roger Penrose, "Mathematics, the mind, and the physical world."

31. Albert Einstein, *Sidelights on Relativity*, trans. G.B. Jeffery and W. Perrett (London: Methuen & Co., 1922), 28.

32. Albert Einstein, "Physics and Reality" (1936), PDF accessed athttp://www.worldscientific.com/worldscibooks/10.1142/4135#t=toc.

33. Albert Einstein, in a letter to Maurice Solovine dated March 30, 1952.

34. Paul Davies, *The Mind of God* (New York: Touchstone, 1992), 150.

35. Davies, *The Mind of God*, 151.

36. Davies, *The Mind of God*, 148.

37. Paul Davies, *Are We Alone?* (New York: Orion Productions, 1995), 85.

38. Paul Davies, *The Goldilocks Enigma* (Boston: Houghton Mifflin, 2008), Kindle Loc. 218.

39. Paul Davies, *The Goldilocks Enigma*.

40. Paul Davies, *The Goldilocks Enigma*, Kindle Loc. 4780.

41. Thomas Nagel, *Mind and Cosmos* (New York: Oxford University Press, 2012), 17.

42. Nagel, *Mind and Cosmos*, 82.

43. Nagel, *Mind and Cosmos*, 121.

44. Thomas Nagel, *The Last Word* (New York: Oxford University Press, 1997), 130.

45. John Lennox, *God's Undertaker: Has Science Buried God?* (Oxford: Lion Books, 2009), 62.

46. John Polkinghorne, *Quantum Physics and Theology: An Unexpected Kinship* (London: Creative Print and Design Group, 2007), 8.

Chapter 10—Mind or Marionette? Rationality and the Existence of the Soul

1. Francis Crick, *The Astonishing Hypothesis: The Scientific Search for the Soul* (New York: Touchstone, 1995), 3.

2. John Searle, *Freedom and Neurobiology* (New York: Columbia University Press, 2006), 5.

3. There is a subtle philosophical distinction between the view that humans *are* souls and the view that humans are composite beings that *have* souls. For the purpose of simplicity, this chapter takes the view that humans *are* souls integrated with a physical body.

4. See J.P. Moreland, *The Soul* (Chicago: Moody Publishers, 2014).

5. Moreland, *The Soul*, 122-123.

6. Moreland, *The Soul*, 34.

7. Steve Volk, "Rewiring the Brain to Treat OCD," *Discover Magazine* (November 2013).

8. Moreland, *The Soul*, 129.

9. Sam Harris, *Free Will* (New York: Free Press, 2012), 5.

10. Blaise Pascal, *Pensées*, Great Books of the Western World, vol. 30 (Chicago: Encyclopaedia Britannica, Inc., 1990), 184.

11. Pascal, *Pensées*, Great Books of the Western World, 234.

12. Thomas Nagel, *The View from Nowhere* (New York: Oxford University Press, 1986), 111.

13. Richard Rorty, *Philosophy and the Mirror of Nature* (Princeton: Princeton University Press, 2009), 387.

14. See Jaegwon Kim, *Physicalism or Something Near Enough* (Princeton: Princeton University Press, 2005).

15. Moreland, *The Soul*, 131.

16. Sir Arthur Eddington, "The Decline of Determinism" in *Great Essays in Science*, ed. Martin Gardner (Amherst, NY: Prometheus Books, 1994), 270-271.

17. Thomas Reid, *Essays on the Intellectual Powers of Man* (Cambridge: John Bartlett, 1852), 5.

18. Reid, *Essays on the Intellectual Powers of Man*, 290.

19. J.B.S. Haldane, *The Inequality of Man* (London: Chatto & Windus, 1932), 162.

20. Hermann Weyl, *Mind and Nature* (Princeton: Princeton University Press, 2009), 52.

21. J.P. Moreland, *The Recalcitrant Imago Dei* (London: SCM Press, 2009), 74.

22. Angus J.L. Menuge, "Why Not Physicalism? The Soul Has Work to Do," unpublished manuscript delivered at the Evangelical Philosophical Society panel for the Society of Biblical Literature, San Francisco, CA, November 2011.

23. Roger Trigg, *Beyond Matter* (West Conshohocken, PA: Templeton Press, 2015), 64-65.

24. Trigg, *Beyond Matter*, 119-120.

25. Quoted from private email correspondence with J.P. Moreland.

Chapter 11—The Maker Thesis: Putting the Pieces Together

1. Athanasius, *Contra Gentes*, paragraph 42.

2. Michael Ramsey, *The Anglican Spirit* (New York: Seabury Classics, 2004), 20.

3. G.K. Chesterton, *Orthodoxy* (Amazon Digital Services, LLC, 2010), 115.

4. G.K. Chesterton, "The Return of the Angels," *Daily News*, March 14, 1903.

5. Chesterton, *Orthodoxy*, 115.

6. Alister McGrath, *Re-Imagining Nature* (Oxford: John Wiley & Sons, 2017), 120.

7. C.S. Lewis, "Is Theology Poetry?" in *The Weight of Glory* (New York: HarperOne, 2000), 140.

Other Good Harvest House Reading

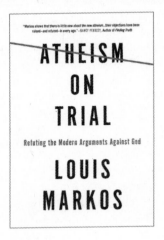

Atheism on Trial
Louis Markos

Atheists are launching a new wave of attacks against Christianity and faith in God. It's hard to know how to handle their claims that they have a more enlightened, scientific, and sophisticated worldview. How can you respond with precision to arguments against your faith?

Dr. Louis Markos confronts the modern-day atheists' claims that new evidence disproves the existence of God. In fact, the "proof" they peddle is not new at all. Rather, they recycle claims that have already been disproven by Christian thinkers of the past.

Equip yourself to defend your beliefs, and stand in confidence that the trial of public opinion versus universal truth has already been held—and God is the victor.

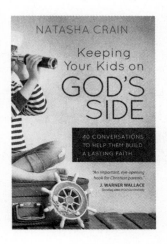

Keeping Your Kids on God's Side

Natasha Crain

It's no secret that children of all ages are being exposed to negative criticism of Christianity as they spend time at school, with friends, or online. Are you prepared to talk with your kids about how they can effectively answer the tough questions that come their way? Here you'll find 40 of the most common challenges kids face—along with clear, easy-to-understand responses you can discuss together.

To learn more about Harvest House books and
to read sample chapters, visit our website:

www.harvesthousepublishers.com

HARVEST HOUSE PUBLISHERS
EUGENE, OREGON